Contents

Dilapidations

RICS guidance note

5th edition

Acknowledgments

Crown copyright material is reproduced with the permission of the Controller of HMSO and the Queen's Printer for Scotland.

The text of the May 2008 edition of the *Pre-action Protocol for Claims for Damages in Relation to the Physical State of Commercial Property at the Termination of a Tenancy* (the 'Dilapidations Protocol') is reproduced with permission from the Property Litigation Association.

Published by the Royal Institution of Chartered Surveyors

Surveyor Court

Westwood Business Park

Coventry CV4 8JE, UK

www.ricsbooks.com

No responsibility for loss or damage caused to any person acting or refraining from action as a result of the material included in this publication can be accepted by the authors or RICS.

Produced by the *Dilapidations Working Group* of the Royal Institution of Chartered Surveyors.

Fourth edition published 2003

ISBN 978 1 84219 403 4

Typeset in Great Britain by Columns Design Ltd, Reading, Berks

Printed in Great Britain by Blackmore Limited, Longmead, Shaftesbury, Dorset

Appendices

RICS guidance notes

This is a guidance note. It provides advice to RICS members on aspects of their practice. Where procedures are recommended for specific professional tasks, these are intended to embody 'best practice', i.e. procedures which in the opinion of RICS meet a high standard of professional competence.

Members are not required to follow the advice and recommendations contained in the note. They should, however, note the following points.

When an allegation of professional negligence is made against a surveyor, the court is likely to take account of the contents of any relevant guidance notes published by RICS in deciding whether or not the surveyor had acted with reasonable competence.

In the opinion of RICS, a member conforming to the practices recommended in this note should have at least a partial defence to an allegation of negligence by virtue of having followed those practices. However, members have the responsibility of deciding when it is inappropriate to follow the guidance.

On the other hand, it does not follow that members will be adjudged negligent if they have not followed the practices recommended in this note. It is for each surveyor to decide on the appropriate procedure to follow in any professional task. However, where a member departs from the practice recommended in this note, he or she should do so only for a good reason. In the event of litigation, the court might require the member to explain why he or she has decided not to adopt the recommended practice. Also, if a member has not followed this guidance, and his or her actions are called into question in an RICS disciplinary case, that member will be asked to justify the steps he or she did take and this may be taken into account.

In addition, guidance notes are relevant to professional competence in that each surveyor should be up to date and should have informed him or herself of guidance notes within a reasonable time of their promulgation.

1 Introduction

1.1 The purpose of this guidance note is to provide practical guidance to RICS members when instructed in connection with dilapidations matters in England and Wales.

1.2 The guidance note seeks to advise members on the factors they should take into consideration when taking their client's instructions, reviewing the lease and other relevant documents, inspecting the subject property, and producing and responding to schedules and other documentation for use by the client, the other party to the lease, third parties, the courts and other legal institutions, such as tribunals.

1.3 A dilapidations claim is an allegation of breach of contract and as such is actionable in law.

1.4 When advising a client on dilapidations matters, a surveyor should seek fully to understand the client's position, the reasons why the surveyor's advice is sought and the use to which that advice might be put. The surveyor should try to ascertain the relevant factual and legal background insofar as it will impact on that advice.

1.5 Often, after a surveyor has advised his or her client, a document is sent or disclosed to the other party to the lease, to third parties, or to a court or tribunal. That document can be held out as the product of the surveyor applying his or her training, knowledge and expertise to the matter. The surveyor, whilst complying with his or her client's instructions, should ensure that any such document does not contain statements or assertions that the surveyor knows or ought to know are not true or properly sustainable or arguable.

1.6 Surveyors should not allow their professional standards to be compromised in order to advance clients' cases. A surveyor should not allow a document that contains statements or assertions that he or she knows or ought to know are not true or properly sustainable or arguable to be sent bearing his or her name or the name of his or her firm. A surveyor should give proper advice even though the client might choose to ignore it.

1.7 **Areas covered**

The situations in which surveyors can be asked to act or advise and which are covered by this guidance note are as follows:
- claims at the end of the term;
- claims during the term;
- forfeiture situations;
- entry to repair situations;
- break clause situations; and
- claims by tenants against landlords.

1.8 **Naming conventions**

1.8.1 Whilst in general this text is gender neutral, on occasions where masculine terms only are used (such as in legislation quotes) these should be taken, in the case of surveyors, as meaning 'she' and 'her' as well, and in the case of the parties, as 'he', 'she', 'they' or 'it' (for the case of a corporate body).

1.8.2 The word 'tribunal' is used to mean courts, tribunals, arbitrators and independent experts.

1.8.3 The physical subject of the claim is referred to as the 'property', which therefore should be taken to include part of a property or a demise.

1.8.4 The *Civil Procedure Rules* apply to the civil courts of England and Wales are referred to as the 'CPR'.

1.8.5 The Pre-Action Protocol of the Property Litigation Association (PLA) (see Appendix A) is referred to as 'The Protocol'.

2 Role of the surveyor

2.1 Generally

2.1.1 A surveyor could be offered instructions in a dilapidations case as an expert witness, and/or as an adviser.

2.1.2 Professional objectivity is required in both the role of adviser and expert witness and in the various types of advice given. The surveyor should act in accordance with the RICS Rules of Conduct.

2.1.3 The surveyor should also note that, pursuant to paragraphs 4.1 to 4.10 of the CPR Practice Direction to Pre-Action Protocols, parties to a dispute:
- are expected to act reasonably in exchanging information and documents to try to avoid litigation;
- should set out in writing the detail of their respective positions; and
- should consider whether some form of alternative dispute resolution would be more suitable than litigation.

2.1.4 The surveyor should guard against exaggeration or understatement. This is particularly important as any subsequent litigation carries with it the danger of a heavy costs order against the party who exaggerates or understates its position. The surveyor should be aware that, pursuant to Part 44.3 of the CPR, the court has discretion as to whether costs are payable by one party to another:

> 'In deciding what order (if any) to make about costs, the court must have regard to all the circumstances, including [inter alia] the conduct of all the parties.'

2.1.5 The rules go on to say that:
> 'The conduct of the parties includes:
> (a) conduct before, as well as during, the proceedings, and in particular the extent to which the parties followed any relevant pre-action protocol;
> (b) whether it was reasonable for a party to raise, pursue or contest a particular allegation or issue;

(c)	the manner in which a party has pursued or defended his case or a particular allegation or issue; and

(d)	whether a claimant who has succeeded in his claim, in whole or in part, exaggerated his claim.'

The above material is reproduced from CPR 44.3(4) and (5). Crown copyright material is reproduced with the permission of the Controller of HMSO and the Queen's Printer for Scotland.

2.1.6	Surveyors should be mindful that the area of dilapidations involves many legal considerations and should avoid advising or taking steps outside their area of expertise.

## 2.2	Acting as adviser (but not instructed as an expert witness)

2.2.1	Surveyors appointed as advisers have an obligation to act in accordance with the RICS Rules of Conduct and their duties to their clients.

2.2.2	The role of adviser can encompass surveyors using their expertise to identify or comment on breaches of covenant and appropriate remedies, prepare schedules or responses, provide or comment on valuation advice, negotiate with other parties with the aim of achieving a settlement, and provide advice on strategy and tactics in relation to a claim or potential claim.

2.2.3	Surveyors should undertake their instructions in an objective, professional manner. They should have appropriate experience and expertise to undertake the instruction. Schedules or responses should not contain allegations of breaches that do not exist, remedies that are inappropriate or costs that are exaggerated or understated.

2.2.4	Surveyors should heed the warning expressed in 2.1.4 regarding exaggeration or understatement, whether in terms of the content of the schedule, the costs attributed to the claim or the overall assessment of loss.

2.2.5	An adviser using his or her expertise to prepare or comment on a schedule or a valuation is not an expert witness. The *Expert Witness* Practice Statement (see 2.3 below) will not therefore apply until the surveyor is considering accepting expert witness instructions. Nonetheless, the surveyor should be influenced by the considerations relating to expert witnesses in advising his or her client, particularly to provide objective advice.

2.2.6	It is also important that surveyors do not formalise settlements without the consent and authority of clients. Indeed, in some situations, it might be appropriate – or a client requirement – that the settlement is formalised via solicitors. See section 12 (*Settlements*).

## 2.3	Expert witness

2.3.1	An expert witness appointment is a personal one. A surveyor appointed as an expert witness (whether appearing for one party or as a single joint expert) will be bound by the RICS Practice Statement and Guidance Note *Surveyors Acting as Expert Witnesses.* Under that Practice Statement and Guidance Note, and also under the CPR where it applies, the surveyor's duty to his or her client is overridden by his or her duty to the tribunal.

2.3.2 Briefly stated, the obligation of an expert witness to any tribunal is to give objective unbiased evidence. It follows that the evidence given by the expert witness should be the same whether acting for the tenant, the landlord or as a single joint expert.

2.3.3 In the context of court proceedings, surveyors' obligations are set out in Part 35 of the CPR and its accompanying Practice Direction.

2.3.4 Surveyors appointed as expert witnesses should also act in accordance with the RICS Rules of Conduct insofar as there is no conflict with their duty to the tribunal.

3 Taking instructions

3.1 Generally

3.1.1 Instructions relating to dilapidations should be taken in accordance with RICS Rules of Conduct. Particular regard should be paid to notification of terms and conditions of engagement to be provided in writing to the client. Instructions in dilapidations matters are no different in this respect from any other instruction.

3.1.2 Surveyors should bear in mind that, in addition to their duties to their clients, they have duties to RICS (in maintaining the reputation of the Institution and complying with its rules). Surveyors will usually also have duties to any tribunals to which they give evidence.

3.1.3 Surveyors should inform clients of these additional duties.

3.1.4 Surveyors may want to consider with each client whether subconsultants are required or may be required during the course of the instruction.

3.2 Fees

3.2.1 Fees for undertaking dilapidations instructions are a matter of contractual agreement between surveyors and their clients.

3.2.2 Surveyors also have an obligation to set out the basis of their fees in such a way that clients are aware of any financial commitments they are making by instructing the surveyor.

3.2.3 As regards conditional/contingency fees for instructions to act as an expert witness, surveyors should take note of the position and guidance set out in *Surveyors Acting as Expert Witnesses* (RICS Practice Statement and Guidance Note).

4 The lease and other enquiries

4.1 The surveyor should obtain a copy of the relevant lease and other documentation with all plans and other attachments.

4.2 Additional information which might be necessary or desirable can include:
- scaled plans;

- licences or other consents for alterations, with plans and specifications;
- any agreement for lease (if intended to survive the grant of the lease);
- assignments and licences to assign;
- side letters or other written agreements;
- schedules of condition, together with appropriate photographs;
- inventories;
- schedules of fixtures and fittings;
- any notices under the *Landlord and Tenant Act* 1954;
- any applications for consent.

4.3   Surveyors should satisfy themselves that the documentation obtained is sufficient for them to discharge their instructions. Any questions as to authenticity need to be addressed to the client or the client's legal adviser. Ambiguities in the documents or in instructions should be clarified as they arise.

4.4   Surveyors should read and seek to understand the documentation to at least a sufficient extent to enable them to discharge their instructions. Surveyors who are uncertain about any item contained in the document, such as the interpretation of a particular covenant or the extent of the property, should bring the matter to the attention of the client or the client's legal advisers.

4.5   **Particular lease clauses to which the surveyor will refer include those listed below.**

4.5.1   *Demise*

Generally a tenant's obligations are limited to the property that has been demised to it. Further, a landlord's obligation to repair, if there is one, will usually be limited to those areas not required to be repaired by the tenant. The surveyor should understand what is the physical subject matter of the relevant covenants.

4.5.2   *Repair*

Repairing covenants vary widely. Some covenants say nothing more than that the property is to be kept in good repair. Others, prepared using the 'torrential' form of drafting, contain a long list of additional requirements, such as to uphold, maintain, rebuild, renew, amend, etc. In whatever manner the covenant is drafted, its scope should be understood thoroughly.

4.5.3   *Decoration*

If there is an obligation to decorate, it might be contained in a separate covenant or might be included as part of the repair covenant. It is usual, but by no means universal, for there to be an obligation to decorate at specific intervals or on particular dates during the term, as well as within some period (usually specified) shortly before the end of the term.

4.5.4   *Alterations and reinstatement*

The surveyor should have regard to both the lease and any licences for alterations when considering the question of alterations and reinstatement. Either or both documents might contain provisions relevant to the surveyor's instructions. An obligation to reinstate lawful alterations will only arise if there is express provision in the lease or licence which may or may not require prior notice to be served. If there is a requirement for prior notice, that notice must be served in compliance with any associated conditions if the obligation is to be enforceable.

4.5.5 *Yielding up*

The 'yield up' clause might simply require the property to be yielded up in accordance with the lease covenants. It might, however, impose a different set of obligations (e.g. complete recarpeting regardless of the condition of the existing carpeting). If the clause is relevant to the surveyor's instructions, that is to say, the lease is shortly to end or has ended, the clause should be considered carefully.

4.5.6 *Statutory obligations*

Leases normally include covenants requiring the tenant to comply with and carry out works required by the provisions of any relevant statute or regulation. Many statutory obligations (e.g. fire regulations) arise only in respect of occupied premises and are not often applicable retrospectively. The surveyor should consider, not just the lease covenant, but the actual provisions of the relevant statute or regulation, or take legal advice on those provisions, if the surveyor believes they are relevant to his or her instructions.

4.6 Recovery of fees

4.6.1
As a general principle, the fees incurred by a landlord for preparing and serving a schedule of dilapidations cannot be recovered from the tenant. Those fees might, however, be recovered pursuant to an express provision in the lease or pursuant to statutory provisions (e.g. section 146 of the *Law of Property Act 1925*). The surveyor should consider the lease to see whether it contains an express recovery provision.

4.6.2
With regard to negotiation fees, if no litigation is commenced and the lease contains no express provision regarding the recovery by the landlord of such fees (as is often the case), then, if the landlord is to make recovery of those fees, they will need to be dealt with as part of the settlement agreement. If, however, litigation is commenced, on the conclusion of the substantive proceedings it would be open to the landlord to seek an order from the court to allow it to recover its negotiation fees.

4.6.3
As to the amount of those negotiation fees, it is common to see as part of a landlord's claim (prior to the commencement of any negotiations) an entry for negotiation fees calculated by reference to the old RICS Scale Fees (now no longer applicable) or some other percentage calculation. Unless the lease expressly provides for recovery on that basis, such claims should be avoided as the fees claimed may bear little or no relationship to the amount of work actually undertaken for which the tenant could reasonably be held to be liable. It is better practice to state that the landlord's claim for negotiation fees are 'to be assessed' or, if a specific figure is included, to state that the figure is an estimate based upon an anticipated level of work.

4.6.4
Other fees might be recoverable, either under the terms of the lease, as consequential losses, or as litigation costs.

4.7   Schedules of condition

The usual purpose of a schedule of condition, when attached to a lease, is to modify or clarify the repairing obligation. There is no standard approach for dealing with such schedules. All that can be said is that the surveyor should consider carefully the drafting of the schedule and the references to it in the body of the lease. If there is any uncertainty as to its application to the surveyor's instructions, the client should be informed of the need for legal input.

4.8   Other enquiries

The other investigations that should be made, and documents gathered, by the surveyor might, depending on the nature of the client's instructions, include the following:

- current or historic planning consents and the planning environment;
- statutory notices relating to the property;
- original or current letting or investment sale details;
- the landlord's intentions for the property at, or shortly after, the termination of the tenancy (this might include details of works proposed to the premises); and
- evidence of rental values and yields.

5   Inspection

5.1   Whenever an inspection is to be undertaken before the lease expires, whether the tenant is in occupation or not, a landlord's surveyor should comply with the terms of the lease when making arrangements for access. (NB: A surveyor who is instructed in connection with a forfeiture situation should check with the client or the client's legal advisers before making access arrangements, to ensure that no issue of waiver of forfeiture rights will arise from making such arrangements.)

5.2   Surveyors are advised to acquaint themselves with RICS guidance relating to inspecting property.

5.3   It is generally appropriate for an independent inspection to be undertaken on behalf of each party initially, although at least one subsequent joint inspection is normally advisable as part of the negotiation dialogue.

5.4   It is advisable for the surveyor, at the time of the initial inspection, to note the general standard of repair in the locality and whether similar properties are empty or boarded up. It is also advisable to note any changes to the nature of the area since the lease was granted. The information might be relevant to the assessment of the scope and standard of repair and also to matters relating to the diminution in the value of the landlord's reversion discussed later. See section 7 (*Claims at the end of the term*).

5.5   The inspection should be sufficiently thorough to enable an accurate record of the relevant breaches to be ascertained. The information recorded should also include all necessary data to allow costs to be calculated. All site notes, measurements or other transcriptions should be retained. When relevant, sketches with a north point should be made and photographs taken. It is recommended that these be cross-referenced to the schedule and dated. If a video record is made, the same would apply.

5.6   Further specialist input might be required from, for example, a consultant engineer or quantity surveyor. The surveyor can facilitate the process, liaising with the client and the consultant(s) concerned as necessary. It is recommended that the surveyor advise the client of the importance of ensuring that the consultants' instructions are consistent with those of the surveyor and that the documentation produced by the consultants is similarly consistent.

5.7   A note might need to be made where further investigation or opening up is required. When this is justified, the agreement of the client and, where appropriate, the tenant should be obtained, together with the extent of making good. It should be noted that, if no breaches are discovered, then the cost of specialist inspections might not be recoverable as part of the claim.

6   The schedule

6.1   Schedules are a record of breaches of covenant. A schedule could be required in each of the situations covered by this guidance note and listed in 1.7 above. Whilst the format will vary depending on the precise situation, schedules should contain these details:

- the contract, lease or covenant alleged to be breached; and
- the nature of the alleged breach.

6.2   Considerations specific to particular uses of schedules in different scenarios are dealt with in the relevant sections of this guidance note. The following are general points.

6.3   **Layout and format**

6.3.1   Scheduled items could be best sorted into sections relating to the type of covenant alleged to have been breached, such as items of repair, decoration, reinstatement and statutory compliance.

6.3.2   Schedules for claims at the end of the term would normally contain the following columns:

- an itemised numbered reference;
- the relevant clause of the lease or other document;
- the breach alleged;
- the remedy required; and
- the cost of the remedy.

6.3.3   The columns in other schedules can vary depending on the purpose of the schedule.

6.3.4   An example of a schedule of dilapidations is attached at Appendix B.

6.4   **Costing**

6.4.1   The schedule of dilapidations should be costed if it is anticipated that the appropriate remedy is damages. There will also be other situations where the parties will require costing of the schedule. In any such case, the schedule should be priced with due reference to reliable and appropriate cost information which is available from a number of sources, for example:

- current Building Cost Information Service data and other recognised price books (to which the appropriate regional variations should be applied);
- relevant and recent tender price information (on projects of a similar nature and size to that envisaged by the claim); and
- the result of a consultation with and assistance from a contractor (which could be conducted on the basis of a full specification of works derived from the schedule of dilapidations).

6.4.2 Pricing should be undertaken in sufficient detail to enable an itemised breakdown of the costs to be provided in the event that the recipient of the claim challenges the quantum.

6.4.3 For larger and more complicated claims it could be appropriate for the client to engage a quantity surveyor to undertake the pricing process, the cost of which might be recoverable as part of the cost of preparing the schedule, if preparation costs are themselves recoverable (see 4.6 above).

6.5   Service

6.5.1 The claimant's solicitor will usually formally 'serve' the schedule of dilapidations, perhaps because legal and statutory formalities apply.

6.5.2 Where formal 'service' is not necessary it can be quite acceptable for the landlord's surveyor to simply issue this document on a client's behalf. In such instances, surveyors should advise clients to satisfy themselves by consultation with their solicitors that the formal route is not required. In each case, confirmation should be obtained from the client of the address to which the schedule should be sent.

6.6   The schedule in discussions

6.6.1 In most instances, the claim is discussed between the parties with a view to reaching a negotiated settlement. By adding additional columns to the schedule both parties can record their respective positions thereby developing it into a Scott Schedule.

6.6.2 An example of a Scott Schedule is attached at Appendix D.

6.6.3 During the course of dialogue, the tenant's surveyor can generally state his or her position on the above basis by use of the columns entitled 'tenant's comments' and 'tenant's costs'. Thereafter, the construction of any subsequent schedules will be largely a matter of common sense, reflecting how the surveyors agree the dialogue should be recorded in the interests of narrowing the issues between them.

6.7   The schedule in proceedings

6.7.1 If the dispute is not resolved and proceedings are commenced, the claim is most likely to be based upon the schedules prepared by the surveyor. The version of the schedule is likely to be the one following discussions with the defendant so that the most up to date position is put before the tribunal. This is likely to be in Scott Schedule form so that the views of the defendant are also shown to the tribunal.

6.7.2 Surveyors should be aware of the wide scope of the courts' powers on costs under the CPR. It is possible that the schedule originally served, or the original response will be compared with that forming the basis of the claim or defence and the finally determined liability. If the original schedule is found to be exaggerated, or the original response found to be understated, the offending party will be at risk of a punitive order on costs.

7   Claims at the end of the term

7.1 Probably the most common dilapidations situation is where:

- a lease has ended or is close to ending; and
- the property has been, or it is anticipated that it will be, left in a condition below covenanted condition.

7.2 If the lease has already ended, the only remedy a landlord has is a claim for damages.

7.3 If the surveyor is instructed before the lease has ended, there can be alternative remedies available to the landlord. These alternatives are discussed in section 8 of this guidance note (*Claims during the term*). Further, there might be time for the tenant to comply with the terms of the lease. The surveyor should consider these alternative remedies, bearing in mind that damages will become the only remedy once the lease expires.

7.4 Schedules served by landlords in respect of claims at the end of the term are commonly known as 'terminal schedules' or 'final schedules'.

7.5 **Principles of damages**

7.5.1 A landlord cannot recover more than its loss. The purpose of damages is to compensate an injured party for its loss; it is not to punish. That is the position regardless of the nature of the breach(es).

7.5.2 As a consequence of the common law and statutory positions described below, generally, the damages recovered by a landlord will be agreed or determined by reference to:

- the cost of works;
- the diminution in the value of the landlord's reversion; or
- a combination of the two.

7.5.3 How that loss is assessed is discussed in section 7.6 below.

7.5.4 The common law position is that, where there has been a breach of the repair covenant, the normal measure of damages is the cost of repair. By virtue of statute, namely, section 18(1) of the *Landlord and Tenant Act* 1927, a landlord cannot recover more than the diminution in the value of its reversion.

7.5.5 Note that section 18(1) of the *Landlord and Tenant Act* 1927 only applies to repair covenants and has two parts or 'limbs'. The 'first limb', which applies to both claims at the end of the term and claims during the term, provides that the damages recovered for breach of a repair covenant cannot exceed the diminution in the value of the landlord's reversion. The 'second limb', which applies only to claims at the end of the term, provides that no damages are recoverable if the property is to be demolished or structural alterations undertaken that would render valueless the repairs the tenant should have undertaken.

7.5.6 Where there have been breaches of covenants other than the repair covenant, damages are usually assessed at common law by reference to the diminution in the value of the landlord's reversion but, in an appropriate case, can be assessed by reference to the cost of works.

7.6 Assessment of loss

7.6.1 It is usual for the landlord's loss at the termination date of the lease to be assessed by reference to the cost of works. Whether the unadjusted cost of works properly reflects that loss will depend on a number of factors, including:

- the landlord's intentions for the property;
- whether the landlord has carried out, or intends to carry out, the works;
- whether the property has potential for redevelopment or refurbishment;
- the market for the property; and
- what arrangements might be made with a new tenant.

The cost of repair figure might only be a starting point from which adjustments need to be made. Those adjustments are known by various names, including 'dilutive effects' and 'supersession'.

Adjustments to cost of works

7.6.2 Where the landlord has carried out, or intends to carry out, all the works that the tenant failed to complete, the cost of works could represent the landlord's loss and no adjustment might be required.

7.6.3 If, however, the landlord has not done and does not intend to do some or any of the works, the cost of works figure might not be a fair reflection of the landlord's loss. The reason for the landlord not doing the works and its intentions for the property might need to be examined. Its intention might be to do works that would have rendered valueless some or all of the items that the tenant failed to carry out and so those items would need to be removed from the schedule and the claim.

7.6.4 In an extreme case, if the landlord intends to demolish the property, few or no items will remain.

7.6.5 Where the property has potential for redevelopment or refurbishment, depending on the circumstances, items of work rendered valueless by this potential may need to be removed to arrive at a fair figure for the landlord's loss.

7.6.6 Where there are several different ways of properly undertaking an item of work but the landlord undertakes or intends to undertake a method that is not the cheapest, there is a risk that the landlord will not be able to recover the full cost.

7.6.7 Where remedial work cannot be undertaken without some degree of betterment or improvement, the full cost will normally be recoverable by the landlord. However, where there are alternative methods, some of which involve betterment or improvement and some of which do not, it is likely that recovery will be limited to the cost of the methods that do not involve betterment.

7.6.8 *Comparable method of assessment*

If the appropriate evidence is available, the landlord's loss could be assessed by:

- ascertaining the market value of the property in the state in which it should have been left by the tenant pursuant to the covenants of the lease; and

- deducting from that the market value of the property in the actual condition in which it was left.

7.7 The Protocol

7.7.1 A surveyor dealing with a claim at the end of the term should be aware of the protocol ('the Protocol') produced by Property Litigation Association ('the PLA'). The PLA website can be found at www.pla.org.uk

7.7.2 The *Civil Procedure Rules* (CPR) in the civil courts of England and Wales encourage the parties to a dispute to exchange full information before proceedings are issued, to enable the parties to avoid litigation where possible and to support the efficient management of proceedings where litigation cannot be avoided. These objectives are addressed by way of pre-action protocols.

7.7.3 The Protocol is one such protocol (though it has yet to be formally adopted under the CPR) and relates to schedules of dilapidations served at the end of the term. Surveyors are encouraged to use it as a guide to good practice and to direct their client's attention to it.

7.8 The lease, other documents and enquiries

7.8.1 The surveyor should obtain and consider the lease and other relevant documents as discussed in section 4 above. In particular, the yield up clause of the lease (see 4.5.5 above) should be considered.

7.8.2 For the reasons outlined in 7.6 above, the intentions of the landlord with regard to the premises at or shortly after the end of the term should be ascertained. It should be established, for example, whether the building is to be demolished or physically altered in any way and if so, in what manner.

7.8.3 For similar reasons, the property's potential for redevelopment or refurbishment should be looked into. Enquiries should also be made of the local planning authority.

7.9 Inspection

It is recommended that the guidance in section 5 above regarding inspections is followed. If the property is inspected before the end of the lease, it should be re-inspected at the end of the lease (see 7.10.4 below).

7.10 Schedule

7.10.1 The guidance in section 6 above regarding schedules should be followed. The surveyor should consider, in particular, paragraph 6.3.1 as to separation of various breaches of covenant. An example of such a schedule of dilapidations is also included in this guidance note at Appendix B.

7.10.2 As a claim at the end of the term is a claim for damages, costings are essential. It is particularly important – and helpful to everyone concerned – if the claim represented by the schedule is fully summarised on a single sheet either at the beginning or the end of the schedule. Cross-references to sections of the schedule, if there is more than one section, are also useful.

7.10.3 Dialogue is inevitable on such claims, and the schedule should be structured so as to aid such dialogue.

7.10.4 It is common practice for an uncosted schedule to be prepared and served by the landlord on the tenant before the end of the term and then, following the expiration of the lease, for a costed schedule to be served. Surveyors should be mindful, however, of the following:

- Which clauses of the lease are alleged to have been breached will depend on the time the schedule is served. Different covenants can easily apply during the term and at the end of the term.

- The property should be re-surveyed at the end of the lease. The condition of the property set out in a schedule served before the end of the term might not be the same as the condition at the end of the term. The condition might be better (if, for example, the tenant has done some remedial work), the same, or worse (perhaps through further deterioration, or damage caused by the tenant's removal activity).

7.10.5 When drafting a schedule of dilapidations for a claim at the end of the term, the surveyor should have regard to the requirements in section 3 *The Schedule* of the Protocol.

7.10.6 The requirements of the Protocol might helpfully be supplemented in some cases. For example, if there are adjustments to the cost of repair for the reasons discussed in 7.6.2 to 7.6.7 above or for any other reason, then it will be helpful for those adjustments to be shown on an item-by-item basis. They could be recorded, perhaps by adding further columns to the schedule, such that the whole nature of the dispute can be considered on an item-by-item basis by the parties and, should the matter go so far, at trial.

7.10.7 Though the surveyor who prepares the schedule might exclude items from the final schedule that is served on the tenant for the reasons discussed in 7.6.2 to 7.6.7 above, it is recommended that he or she makes and keeps a note of all breaches of the lease, as that information might be needed for an assessment of the diminution in the value of the landlord's reversion. That information may also be relevant to the question of costs.

7.11 Surveyor's endorsement

7.11.1 The schedule should be endorsed by the surveyor preparing it. The endorsement can be given either by the surveyor in his or her own name or by the surveyor signing in his or her own name stating he or she does so 'for and on behalf of' XX firm or company if appropriate.

7.11.2 The requirement for the surveyor's written endorsement is found in paragraph 3.6 of the Protocol which specifies that:

> 'The schedule should include an endorsement by the surveyor preparing it. The surveyor's endorsement should confirm that in the opinion of the surveyor all the works set out in the schedule are reasonably required in order to put the premises into the physical state referred to in paragraph 3.1 [of the Protocol]; that full account has been taken of the landlord's intentions for the property at or shortly after the termination of the tenancy; and that the costs, if any, quoted for such works are reasonable.'

The text of paragraph 3.6 of the *Pre-action Protocol for Claims for Damages in Relation to the Physical State of Commercial Property at the Termination of a Tenancy* (the 'Dilapidations Protocol') is reproduced with permission from the Property Litigation Association.

7.11.3 Before giving the endorsement, the surveyor should consider the guidance set out in 1.5 and 1.6 above.

7.11.4 It is recommended that the surveyor asks the landlord for its intentions for the property in writing before making the endorsement (see 4.8 and 7.8.2 above), and that a written record of the reply is made and kept on file.

7.11.5 In giving an endorsement, the surveyor should make reference to any relevant information provided by the landlord or advice given by consultants such as valuers and quantity surveyors.

7.11.6 Before giving the endorsement, if there is a concern as to the landlord's entitlement under the lease to pursue an item, whether in the body of the schedule or a consequential loss item, the surveyor should bring the matter to his or her client's attention and, if necessary, recommend that advice is sought from the client's solicitors.

7.12   Consequential losses

7.12.1 Where relevant, the following consequential losses incurred might be added to the claim:

- legal fees in connection with the service of the schedule;
- administration of the work envisaged by the schedule;
- VAT (see Appendix E);
- holding costs expected to be incurred before re-letting or sale, as the case may be;
- loss of rent until the end of any works and during any additional marketing period required as a consequence;
- rates liability;
- insurance, security, energy and cleaning costs not already reflected in the building works claim;
- loss due to lack of service charge recoupment;
- finance costs (including interest);

also:

- preparation of the schedule; and
- other fees of the surveyors (including fees relating to assessment of rent and diminution in value).

However, the ability to claim these losses could be subject to specific lease requirements.

7.12.2   Paragraph 4.6 of the Protocol requires that the legal basis for claimed consequential losses be set out.

7.13   Statement of loss

7.13.1   The initial pre-action claim by the landlord for damages is dealt with in section 4 of the Protocol. The use in the Protocol of the phrase 'the claim' is a reference to the landlord's formal statement of what it considers it is owed in damages as representing its loss. That statement is made before proceedings are commenced. It is the starting point for the steps that follow and which may or may not lead to court proceedings. The expression 'the claim' is therefore not to be confused with the phrases 'particulars of claim' or 'claim form' which are documents used in court proceedings; the claim is a reference to the whole statement of the landlord's loss in advance of proceedings.

7.13.2   The landlord's pre-action claim for damages should include a full statement of what the landlord says it is owed for the schedule. It will usually consist of a costed schedule of dilapidations (endorsed by the surveyor preparing it, dealt with above in 7.11) and a summary of any consequential losses, together with all the items mentioned at paragraph 4.7 of the Protocol.

7.14   Service

The landlord's initial pre-action claim for damages is usually served on the tenant by the landlord's solicitors. There is generally no formal requirement in the lease for service in that manner, but the lease should be checked. In the absence of any such requirements, the landlord needs simply to convey the claim it is making to the tenant by an effective route.

7.15   The response

7.15.1   In preparing a response, the tenant's surveyor should consider the factors and take many of the steps the landlord's surveyor should have considered and taken as discussed above. The standard of behaviour required of a surveyor is the same whether he or she acts for a landlord or tenant.

7.15.2   The Protocol contains recommended timing for the tenant's response to the claim letter in relation to an end-of-term schedule of dilapidations (56 days), and the subsequent progress of negotiations.

7.16   The Scott Schedule

7.16.1   The landlord's item-by-item claim schedule and the tenant's item-by-item response are usually brought together for ease of reference in a Scott Schedule.

7.16.2 The suggested structure of a Scott Schedule is set out in Appendix C and discussed above at 6.6. The Scott Schedule is indispensable as an aid to dialogue between parties in claims at the end of the term.

7.17 Dialogue

7.17.1 Both the courts and RICS encourage dialogue between parties to a dispute. In order to achieve this, it is desirable that surveyors of like disciplines should meet during the course of the dispute, in order to clarify the nature of the dispute and if possible, to settle aspects of it.

7.17.2 Because of the high costs involved, it should be the parties' objective, as well as the courts', that the matter be settled instead of tried, if at all possible.

7.18 Physical work versus damages

7.18.1 There might be advantages to both landlord and tenant in works being carried out by the tenant prior to the end of the term. From the landlord's perspective, it could be able to market the premises more speedily. Equally, a tenant who chooses to do the work during the term:

- will have control of the actual works and the timetable for those works;
- will probably avoid a claim for loss of rent and interest; and
- might be able to recover VAT where the landlord cannot (see Appendix E).

7.18.2 After the lease has expired, the landlord has control. It will be able to dictate the quality and scope of the works (as far as the expired lease allows), as well as the timetable. The landlord can then recover its loss as damages.

7.19 Court proceedings

7.19.1 Most dilapidations claims at the end of the term do not result in proceedings being issued. Normally the matter can be settled between the parties without that step being taken. Should matters go so far, however, once proceedings are issued, the surveyor will need to take his or her lead from the client's solicitors.

8 Claims during the term

8.1 'Interim claims' is the name often given to claims that do not fall within the definition of claims at the end of the term. A better expression, for clarity of definition, is 'claims during the term'.

8.2 The remedies available to a landlord pursuing a claim during the term can include:

- damages;
- forfeiture;
- entry to carry out the work, followed by a claim for costs; and
- specific performance.

8.3 The remedies of damages, forfeiture and entry to carry out the work are considered below.

8.4   The remedy of specific performance is beyond the scope of this guidance note. Legal advice should be taken in every case.

8.5   The PLA Protocol does not apply to claims during the term. However, paragraphs 4.1 to 4.10 of the CPR Practice Direction to Pre-Action Protocols could apply to such claims. See 2.1.3 above and Appendix G.

8.6   Damages

8.6.1   The *Leasehold Property (Repairs) Act* 1938 (the 1938 Act) will apply to a landlord's claim for damages during the term if the lease was granted for a term of seven years or more and three or more years of the term remain unexpired.

8.6.2   If the 1938 Act applies, the landlord must first serve a notice under section 146 of the *Law of Property Act* 1925 and then, if the tenant serves a counternotice within 28 days of service of the notice, must obtain the permission of the court before commencing proceedings.

8.6.3   As noted in 7.5.1 above, the purpose of damages is to compensate an injured party for its loss; it is not to punish.

8.6.4   With damages claims during the term, the common law position is that, whether there have been breaches of the repair covenant or other breaches of covenant, damages are usually assessed by reference to the diminution in the value of the landlord's reversion.

8.6.5   Where the breach is of the repair covenant, the 'first limb' of section 18(1) of the *Landlord and Tenant Act* 1927 will also apply (see 7.5.5 above). However, given that the cap imposed by that section is the same as the normal measure of damages, it is likely to have little effect on the level of damages recovered.

8.6.6   Where the lease has some time to run before its expiration, the landlord might have some difficulty in establishing any substantial diminution. Exceptions to this can include situations where the landlord owns other nearby or adjoining properties which are being devalued or endangered by the tenant's breaches.

8.7   Forfeiture

8.7.1   The remedy of forfeiture, if successfully pursued, results in the lease coming to an end. This is a complex area. Consequently, it is strongly recommended that legal advice should be obtained.

8.7.2   A landlord cannot forfeit a lease for a tenant's non-compliance with its covenants unless:
- the lease contains a forfeiture clause;
- the landlord has served a valid notice pursuant to section 146 of the *Law of Property Act* 1925 on the tenant;
- a reasonable period of time has expired since service of the section 146 notice; and
- the tenant has not complied with the section 146 notice during that time.

8.7.3   If the lease was granted for a term of seven years or more, of which three years or more remain unexpired, the *Leasehold Property (Repairs) Act* 1938 will again apply. Under the 1938 Act, if the tenant serves a counternotice within the 28 days of service of the section 146 notice, the landlord cannot forfeit the lease without the permission of the court.

8.7.4   Additional restrictions apply to the forfeiture of residential long leases.

8.7.5   The right to forfeit can be lost or waived by a landlord if it or its agents, after becoming aware of the relevant breach, take any step that unequivocally recognises the continuing existence of the lease, such as demanding or accepting rent. The issue of waiver might not be relevant to a continuing breach (such as of a repair covenant) but might be of importance where there has been a once-and-for-all breach (such as making alterations without the requisite consent).

8.8   Entry to undertake remedial works

8.8.1   Many leases contain a right for the landlord to enter the property without the consent of the tenant to undertake works the tenant should have carried out (i.e. where the tenant is in default of its obligations). These are sometimes known as '*Jervis v Harris*' clauses after a prominent legal case.

8.8.2   These clauses are usually very specific about the circumstances under which landlords can operate the rights they contain (such as notice periods for landlord's inspections) and what works are to be undertaken should breaches of covenant be found.

8.8.3   Extreme caution is required when using these clauses. Incorrect application by a landlord can lead to counterclaims from the tenant for trespass and breach of quiet enjoyment. Consequently, it is strongly recommended that legal advice is obtained regarding their use.

8.8.4   Usually, the landlord is entitled to enter the property (subject to specific notice requirements) and to take a record or schedule of the breaches of covenant and then to serve notice of those breaches on the tenant. It is essential that only the breaches allowed for by the clause are scheduled and no others. If the clause only refers to breaches of repairing covenant, only items of repair can be included in the schedule. Incorporation of inappropriate breaches could invalidate later steps under the clause.

8.8.5   Once notice has been served on the tenant, there is usually a specific time period for the tenant to undertake the works. Again, this time period can vary, as can the obligation to complete or commence the works.

8.8.6   If, at the end of the designated time period, the tenant has not undertaken the works set out in the landlord's notice, the landlord is entitled to enter the property and undertake the works itself. The works are only those set out in the landlord's notice in accordance with the terms of the lease.

8.8.7   Normally, the landlord's costs are recoverable as a debt, not as damages, and the provisions of the *Leasehold Property (Repairs) Act* 1938 and section 18(1) of the *Landlord and Tenant Act* 1927 will not apply. However, the clause may provide for the costs to be recoverable as 'liquidated damages' or have some similar wording, in which case it is possible that these statutory provisions will apply.

8.9 Instructions

8.9.1 Refer to section 3 (*Taking instructions*) above.

8.9.2 On being instructed by a party in connection with a claim during the term, the surveyor should also ascertain the remedy or remedies being contemplated or pursued by the landlord and the role the surveyor is to play in pursuing/defending against that remedy/those remedies.

8.10 The lease, other documents and enquiries

8.10.1 Refer to section 4 (*The lease and other enquiries*) above.

8.10.2 Where the landlord is pursuing forfeiture as a remedy, particular note should be made of the forfeiture clause and circumstances in which forfeiture is permitted.

8.10.3 Where the landlord is pursuing a remedy under an entry to repair clause, the terms of the clause should be considered carefully for the reasons set out in 8.8 above.

8.10.4 Any issues of interpretation should be referred to the client's solicitors.

8.11 Inspection

8.11.1 Refer to section 5 (*Inspection*) above.

8.11.2 Surveyors instructed by landlords pursuing forfeiture are reminded in particular of the warning given in 5.1 above about waiver of forfeiture rights.

8.11.3 If the landlord is pursuing a remedy under an entry to repair clause, the surveyor should follow precisely the procedural steps and timings set out in the lease concerning inspections.

8.12 Schedule

8.12.1 Refer to section 6 (*The schedule*) above.

8.12.2 Where the schedule is to be attached to a section 146 notice, where damages and/or forfeiture are being pursued, it should set out the breach. The remedial work can also be set out although, under section 146, it is not strictly necessary to do so.

8.12.3 Where the schedule is produced pursuant to an entry to repair clause, it is similarly likely to be a requirement that breaches be specified rather than the remedy. Regardless of the manner in which the clause is drafted, though, its requirements should be closely followed.

8.12.4 Only if damages are being pursued is it likely to be appropriate for the schedule to be costed and, even then, the costs of works might bear little resemblance to the loss that the landlord has suffered, particularly if the lease has some time to run (see 8.6.6 above).

8.13 Service

It is very likely that, where forfeiture or an entry to repair remedy is being pursued and/or the 1938 Act applies, formal notice provisions will apply. Service should therefore be undertaken by the client's solicitors.

8.14 Response

In preparing a response, the tenant's surveyor should consider the factors, and take many of the steps, that the landlord's surveyor should have considered, and taken, as discussed above.

8.15 Undertaking the work

The tenant might consider undertaking the work to minimise the claim against it or to avoid losing the lease altogether. The surveyor should review the discussion at 7.18 above, which sets out some of the relevant considerations, and should advise his or her client on the possible advantages and disadvantages of undertaking the work.

8.16 Subsequent steps

The subsequent course of the dispute depends on the remedy being pursued by the landlord. If the landlord is pursuing a damages claim, the parties' surveyors might be able to negotiate a settlement without the (further) need for the involvement of solicitors other than, possibly, to document any settlement reached. By contrast, if forfeiture or the use of an entry to repair clause is being pursued, the tenant's reaction to the threatened use of the remedy could require legal advice, as could the manner in which the remedy is to be implemented.

8.17 Court proceedings

Most claims do not result in proceedings being issued. Normally the matter can be settled between the parties without that step being taken. Should matters go so far, however, once proceedings are issued the surveyor will need to take his or her lead from the client's solicitors.

9 Break clauses

9.1 Many leases contain clauses giving either landlord or tenant the right to determine the lease before the end of the contractual term. These are also known as options to determine or, more commonly, break clauses.

9.2 It is strongly recommended that legal advice be obtained when dealing with a break clause.

9.3 Any conditions relating to the exercise of a break must be complied with for the break clause to operate. It is for the party operating the break clause to ensure it has complied with the relevant conditions.

9.4 Conditions often found in leases include the following:

- *Service of a period of notice.* Time can be of the essence when dealing with notice periods. Further, some time periods are precise and specify a particular date by which notice must be served, others give a minimum period of notice such as 'not less than six months'.

- *Payment of a premium.* This obligation could vary in application and could specify either a fixed amount or the method of calculating the amount, such as 'six months' rent'.

- *Providing vacant possession.* This is an obligation on a tenant-operated break clause. Provision of vacant possession implies removal of all tenant's chattels. It is essential that all chattels are removed, and what constitutes a chattel will require careful consideration.

- *Compliance with lease obligations.* This is an obligation on a tenant-operated break clause. The requirements of this clause can vary, so careful reading is required. For example, if full compliance is required there can be no subsisting breaches on the option date. If compliance is qualified in any way, or compliance only with specific covenants is required, whilst the scope/standard might not be so onerous, it is nevertheless recommended that the highest standards are applied when undertaking works.

9.5 If one or more of the conditions attached to a break are not satisfied, the lease will continue past the break date, unless the parties agree otherwise.

9.6 For the surveyor advising on the physical condition of the property, providing vacant possession and compliance with lease obligations are the more relevant considerations. These should be considered in conjunction with the solicitors advising on the legal matters. It is recommended that advice be sought if there is any uncertainty over the obligations or conditions.

9.7 Instruction, lease, enquiries and inspection

9.7.1 It is strongly recommended that a surveyor, on being instructed in connection with a break clause, immediately obtains and reads the lease to make him or herself aware of any relevant time limits and conditions. Many negligence actions have arisen from professional advisers failing to spot such time limits or conditions through not reviewing the lease at an early stage. Extreme care should be taken to ensure that the interplay between the legal position, the landlord's objectives and the physical state of the building is handled correctly; legal advice should be sought on every occasion.

9.7.2 The objectives of the client with regard to the break and the property should also be ascertained, as should the objectives of the other party, insofar as the client is aware of them.

9.7.3 The further steps that are taken by the surveyor will very much depend on the objectives of the client and the client's preferred strategy for dealing with the break. It may or may not be in the client's best interest for the surveyor to inspect the property, to make enquiries of his or her counterpart at an early stage, or to produce a schedule. No steps of this nature should be taken without legal advice.

9.8 Schedule

If the surveyor is instructed by a landlord to produce a schedule in connection with a break clause, the surveyor should consider the guidance given in section 6 above (*The schedule*). If the landlord is seeking to make the tenant aware of the works it considers need to be completed before the break takes effect, it is likely that the schedule will not need to be costed. If, however, the landlord is seeking to agree a financial settlement with the tenant, then it should probably be costed and include a claim for relevant consequential losses. Much of the guidance in section 7 (*Claims at the end of the term*) could also be of relevance.

9.9 Service

It could be that formal notice of the break has already been served and that the lease contains no further service requirements. Nevertheless, the surveyor should consider with the client's solicitors the manner in which any schedule the surveyor is instructed to produce is served on the tenant.

9.10 Response

The response by a tenant to the receipt (or non-receipt, for that matter) of a schedule will depend on the tenant's objectives and preferred strategy for dealing with the break. The guidance above should also be considered by the surveyor instructed by a tenant.

9.11 Dialogue and court proceedings

The nature and extent of any dialogue will depend on the parties' objectives and strategies. The surveyor is reminded that the courts and RICS encourage parties to be open and reasonable in the manner in which they conduct themselves in disputes and that, where parties fail to be open or they conduct themselves in an unreasonable manner and matters proceed to court, they could suffer cost sanctions.

10 Claims against landlords

10.1 A lease can contain a landlord's covenant to repair the property and/or other parts of the building (e.g. the common parts) or such an obligation might be implied by statute or common law.

10.2 Generally, a tenant cannot enforce a landlord's covenant/obligation to repair within the property unless the tenant has first given the landlord notice of the breach. In respect of repairs outside the property (e.g. within the common parts of the building), generally no notice is required.

10.3 For evidential reasons, any notice required should be in writing. The landlord does not need to be given exact details of the disrepair, or of the remedial works required, so long as the contents are sufficient to put the landlord on notice that works are required.

10.4 In addition to carrying out works of repair for which it is liable, the landlord will generally be obliged to make good any consequential damage to the property caused by such works of repair.

10.5 Remedies

10.5.1 The remedies available to a tenant for breach by the landlord of its repairing obligation include:

- damages;
- self-help; and
- set-off.

10.5.2 There could be other remedies available (e.g. specific performance) but these are beyond the scope of this guidance note.

Damages

10.5.3 As before, whilst an award of damages is one of a number of possible remedies available during the term, it is the only remedy available at the end of the term.

10.5.4 Section 18(1) of the *Landlord and Tenant Act* 1927 does not apply to a tenant's claim for damages.

10.5.5 The amount of damages to which a tenant is entitled is that which, so far as money can, will put the tenant in the position in which he or she would have been had there been no breach by the landlord.

10.5.6 Where there has been a breach of the landlord's repair covenant, the tenant may choose to:

- remain in the property;
- temporarily vacate; or
- sell its interest in the property or sublet.

10.5.7 The appropriate heads of damages will vary depending on which of these actions the tenant takes.

10.5.8 A tenant who remains in the property might claim for:

- inconvenience and discomfort (which might be assessed by reference to the rental value of the premises);
- ill health;
- damage to personal belongings;
- damage to the property; and/or
- loss of profits.

10.5.9 A tenant who vacates might claim for:

- cost of alternative accommodation;
- cost of moving;
- redecoration and cleaning costs; and/or
- loss of profits.

10.5.10 A tenant who sells or sublets might claim for any reduction in price/rent achieved due to the breach.

Self-help

10.5.11 Where the breach relates to part of the property, the tenant can carry out the required works itself and seek to recover the cost from the landlord. Where it relates to disrepairs outside the property (e.g. within the common parts of the building), in the absence of an express right, the tenant should be cautious about undertaking the work itself. There could be no implied right of entry, and the tenant could be committing a trespass.

Set-off

10.5.12 Set-off is deduction from rent and other sums payable to the landlord under the lease. The tenant might wish to recover the damages it has suffered by way of set-off, along with any sum the tenant has reasonably spent remedying the breach through self-help.

10.5.13 The right of set-off can, however, be expressly excluded by the terms of the lease.

10.6   Instructions, documentation and inspection

10.6.1 On being instructed by a party to a claim by a tenant against a landlord, the surveyor should make many of the same enquiries and take most of the steps that would have been made and taken in a claim by a landlord against a tenant, as set out in sections 3 to 5 of this guidance note.

10.6.2 Additional matters to note are as follows.

10.6.3 The Protocol does not apply to claims by tenants against landlords. However, paragraphs 4.1 to 4.10 of the CPR Practice Direction to Pre-Action Protocols can apply to such claims. See 2.1.3 above and Appendix G.

10.6.4 The scope of the landlord's repairing covenant could be contained in the service charge provisions, and/or alongside the landlord's other covenants or implied. The covenant/implied obligation should be fully understood, as should any provisions restricting the remedy or remedies available to the tenant.

10.6.5 The surveyor should ascertain what action the tenant has taken following the breach, in terms of remaining in occupation, vacating, selling its interest or subletting.

10.6.6 The surveyor should seek to understand the remedy or remedies being sought or pursued by the tenant.

10.7   Schedule

10.7.1 If the landlord's breach is a simple one (e.g. failure to maintain the communal air-conditioning plant in a multi-let office block), a schedule might not be required. If, however, there are numerous items of breach, then the tenant's claim will be better set out in schedule form.

10.7.2 The schedule used for a claim by a tenant against a landlord is likely to be similar to that required for a claim by a landlord against a tenant. Whether such a schedule should be costed will depend on the remedy or remedies being sought. One prepared where the tenant is proposing self-help probably does not need initially to be costed. One prepared in connection with a damages or set-off claim might need to be, depending on the heads of damage.

10.8   Service

The tenant's claim will usually be served on the landlord by the tenant's solicitors but there is generally no formal requirement in the lease for service in that manner.

10.9   The response

In preparing a response, the landlord's surveyor should consider the factors and take many of the steps the tenant's surveyor should have considered and taken, as discussed above.

10.10   Undertaking the work

The landlord ought to consider undertaking the work to minimise the claim against it. The surveyor should review the discussion at 7.18 above which sets out some of the relevant considerations and should advise his or her client on the possible advantages and disadvantages of this route.

10.11   Subsequent steps

The subsequent course of the dispute depends on the remedy being pursued by the tenant. If the tenant is pursuing a damages and/or set-off claim, it may be that the parties' surveyors can negotiate a settlement without the (further) need for the involvement of solicitors other than, possibly, to document any settlement reached. In contrast, if self-help is being pursued, the landlord's reaction to the threatened use of the remedy could require legal advice, as could the manner in which the remedy is to be implemented.

10.12   Court proceedings

Most claims by tenants against landlords do not result in proceedings being issued. Normally the matter can be settled between the parties without that step being taken. Should matters go so far, however, once proceedings are issued, the surveyor will need to take his or her lead from the client's solicitors.

11   Alternative dispute resolution

11.1   The majority of dilapidations disputes are resolved between the parties. The advent of the CPR and the Protocol has increased the number of disputes resolved this way. However, where disputes cannot be resolved by agreement, it could be necessary to have recourse to litigation.

11.2   Pursuant to the CPR, the court – not the parties – will actively manage the case listed for hearing. In so doing, the court will usually encourage the parties to use an alternative dispute resolution procedure ('ADR') procedure that might offer distinct advantages over litigation, such as speed, privacy, informality and cost.

11.3   ADR is described in the glossary to the CPR as the 'collective description of methods of resolving disputes otherwise than through the normal trial process'. The most widely used are mediation and independent expert determination. Arbitration is also a form of ADR and will often be found to be the required tribunal for resolving certain disputes arising out of leases, such as those pertaining to service charges.

11.4 Unlike arbitration (where the award issued by the arbitrator is based on the evidence adduced by the parties or obtained by enquiry), an independent expert determination is, as the name suggests, a determination by an expert in the field. The expert must base that decision on his or her own knowledge and experience, and is not obliged to receive, or even consider, any evidence adduced by the parties (unless the lease so requires or the parties agree).

11.5 The independent expert's decision, known as a determination, is final and binding, and there is no right of appeal. However, the independent expert can be held liable in damages for any provable loss sustained by a party through the expert's negligence.

11.6 There are several factors that make mediation different from most other forms of dispute resolution:
- No decision can be imposed upon the parties by the mediator; nor will the mediator express any personal view on the dispute unless the parties so request.
- During mediation the parties are able to freely discuss the strengths and weaknesses of their case and those of the other side with the mediator, without prejudicing their position should a settlement not be reached.
- The mediator will also encourage and help the parties to generate and consider their options, and develop these into viable courses of action.

11.7 Further information on ADR can be obtained through the RICS Dispute Resolution Service, which also maintains a register of accredited mediators and a panel of independent experts who are experienced in the field of dilapidations.

12 Settlements

12.1 Most claims do not end up in court. They are normally settled by negotiation. Those negotiations will often be undertaken by the surveyor who acted as adviser and prepared or responded to the original schedule or valuation. In reaching a settlement the surveyor should consider the claim as a whole, including time and costs in pursuing the claim. He or she should bear in mind that the total costs to both parties in relation to a claim taken through to trial will often exceed the value of the claim. It is therefore important that the surveyor provides objective advice on the merits of a proposed settlement.

12.2 If a claim is determined by a court, an arbitrator, or an independent expert, the successful party will have a court order, award or determination which can be enforced by a court. If court proceedings are settled out of court, the terms of the settlement will usually be recorded at the court by way of a court order and hence the proceedings are disposed of. Again, the successful party has a court order which can be enforced.

12.3 However, if a claim for dilapidations is settled between the parties (and most are) either by agreement or by use of a mediator, without court proceedings being issued, the parties must record the terms of the agreement precisely in order that, if necessary, the agreement can be enforced by commencement of court proceedings for breach of the agreement.

12.4   A settlement agreement should:

(a) be in writing, identifying:

- the parties (i.e. the landlord and the tenant);
- the relevant lease;
- the schedule and the claim to which the settlement applies;

(b) be open, i.e. not marked 'without prejudice';

(c) be stated to be in full and final settlement of the claim;

(d) deal with each and every part of the claim including, where appropriate, any interest and costs;

(e) state the date by which:

- if appropriate, any payment pursuant to the agreement is to be paid and/or,
- if appropriate, works are to be conducted, inspected and signed off (including, if appropriate, a procedure for agreement and signing off of any 'snagging items');

(f) be dated; and

(g) be signed by each party, or signed for and on behalf of each party by a duly appointed surveyor, lawyer or agent authorised to bind the party for whom they sign.

Appendices

Appendix A: PLA Protocol

The text of the *Pre-action Protocol for Claims for Damages in Relation to the Physical State of Commercial Property at the Termination of a Tenancy* (the 'Dilapidations Protocol') is reproduced with permission from the Property Litigation Association. The Protocol can also be accessed via the PLA website: www.pla.org.uk

PROPERTY LITIGATION ASSOCIATION PRE-ACTION PROTOCOL FOR CLAIMS FOR DAMAGES IN RELATION TO THE PHYSICAL STATE OF COMMERCIAL PROPERTY AT THE TERMINATION OF A TENANCY (THE 'DILAPIDATIONS PROTOCOL')

May 2008

1   **Introduction**

1.1   This protocol applies to commercial property situate in England and Wales. There is a separate Pre-Action Protocol for Housing Disrepair cases.

1.2   This protocol relates to claims for damages for dilapidations against tenants at the termination of a tenancy. These are generally referred to as terminal dilapidations claims.

1.3   It is not the purpose of this protocol to define "dilapidations", "repair", "reinstatement" or "redecoration". The work to the property that may be required will depend on the contractual terms of the lease and any other licences or other relevant documents. However, as a guide:

1.3.1   "dilapidations" might be said to be a claim for all breaches of covenant or obligation relating to the physical state of a demised property at the termination of the tenancy, and usually includes items of repair, redecoration and reinstatement;

1.3.2   "repair" might be said to be a reference to a state of disrepair in a property, where there is a legal liability to remedy, or undertake, work to rectify it;

1.3.3   "reinstatement" might be said to be a reference to returning a property to its former state prior to carrying out works of alteration, where there is a legal liability to remedy, or undertake, that work;

1.3.4   "redecoration" might be said to be a reference to a state of general finish or appearance of the property as required by the lease, where there is a legal liability to remedy, or undertake, that work.

1.3.5   The tenant may also be required to carry out other works, for example, renewal, replacement and maintenance. This is not an exhaustive list.

1.4 This protocol is not intended to be an exhaustive or mandatory list of steps or procedures to be followed regardless of the circumstances. Those will be determined by the facts of each case. It is also not intended to be an explanation of the law. In deciding the exact steps and procedures to be adopted regard should also be had to the Overriding Objective as set out in CPR Part 1 and the Practice Direction – Protocols.

1.5 This protocol is intended to improve the pre-action communication between landlord and tenant by establishing a timetable for the exchange of information relevant to a dispute and by setting standards for the content of schedules and claims and, in particular, the conduct of pre-action negotiations.

1.6 Compliance with the protocol should enable both landlords and tenants to make an early informed judgment on the merits of their cases. The aim is to increase the number of pre-action settlements. If proceedings are commenced, the court will be able to treat the standards set out in this protocol as the normal reasonable approach to pre-action conduct when the court considers issues of costs and other sanctions under the CPR. When doing so, the court should be concerned with substantial compliance and not minor departures, e.g. failure by a short period to provide relevant information. In addition, minor departures should not exempt the "innocent" party from following the protocol. The court may also be invited to consider the effect of non-compliance on the other party when deciding whether to impose sanctions.

1.7 In complying with this Protocol the landlord and tenant and their professional advisers should have regard to the common law principles of how loss should be calculated and in relation to repairing covenants, s. 18(1) of the *Landlord and Tenant Act* 1927 ("s. 18(1)") ([Annex] A).

1.8 If the landlord or tenant does not seek professional advice from a surveyor they should still, so far as possible, fully comply with the terms of this Protocol.

1.9 Where more than one surveyor is instructed by either the landlord or the tenant, where appropriate, any endorsement required by this Protocol should be given by one or both of the surveyors as appropriate.

2 Overview of Protocol – General Aim

2.1 The objectives of this protocol are:
 (a) to encourage the exchange of early and full information about the prospective legal claim;
 (b) to enable parties to avoid litigation by agreeing a settlement of the claim before the commencement of proceedings;
 (c) to support the efficient management of proceedings where litigation cannot be avoided.

2.2 A flow chart is attached at Annex B.

THE PROTOCOL

3 The Schedule

3.1 Generally, the landlord shall serve a schedule in the form attached at Annex C. It shall:

(a) indicate the breaches of the tenant's covenants or obligations which have not been remedied at the termination of the tenancy,

(b) state what in the opinion of the landlord or its surveyor is necessary to put the property into the physical state required by the terms of the lease and any licences or other relevant documents, and

(c) the landlord's costings (which may be based on its estimate or on invoices if the works have been done).

3.2   Breaches should be separated into relevant categories, e.g. repair, reinstatement, redecoration, etc., and these should be listed separately in the schedule and should (where appropriate) identify any notices served by the landlord requiring reinstatement works to be undertaken.

3.3   The schedule shall be served within a reasonable time. A "reasonable time" will vary from case to case but generally will be not more than 56 days after the termination of the tenancy.

3.4   The landlord may serve a schedule before the termination of the tenancy. However, if it does so it should confirm either at the termination of the tenancy that the situation remains as in its earlier schedule or serve a further schedule within a reasonable time.

3.5   If possible the schedule should also be provided by way of computer disk or similar form to enable the tenant's comments to be incorporated in the one document.

3.6   The schedule should include an endorsement by the surveyor preparing it. The surveyor's endorsement should confirm that in the opinion of the surveyor all the works set out in the schedule are reasonably required in order to put the premises into the physical state referred to in paragraph 3.1 above; that full account has been taken of the landlord's intentions for the property at or shortly after the termination of the tenancy; and that the costs, if any, quoted for such works are reasonable.

3.7   In giving this endorsement the surveyor should have regard to the principles laid down in the Royal Institution of Chartered Surveyors' Guidance Note on Dilapidations.

4   **The Claim**

4.1   The schedule should set out what the landlord considers to be the breaches, the works required to be done to remedy those breaches and the landlord's costings (see 3 above). The claim should set out and substantiate the monetary sum the landlord is claiming as damages in respect of those breaches. This will include the items in the schedule and also any other items of loss it may wish to claim (see 4.6 below). The claim should be limited to the landlord's actual loss (see 4.8 below).

4.2   The claim should indicate clearly how it has been made up. The claim should be set out separately from the schedule but may be part of the same document.

4.3   If the claim is in a separate document from the schedule then this should also be served within the timescale for service of the schedule (see 3.3 above).

4.4 If the claim is based on the cost of works, it should be fully quantified and substantiated. For example, each item of expenditure should, where possible and/or relevant, be supported by either an invoice or detailed estimate.

4.5 All aspects of the claim including the VAT status of the landlord, if appropriate, should be set out.

4.6 If the claim includes any other losses for example:

    (a) surveyor's fees for preparing the schedule;

    (b) professional or other fees or expenses incurred or to be incurred in connection with the carrying out of the remedial works;

    (c) preliminaries; and

    (d) loss of rent, service charge or insurance rent, these must be set out in detail substantiated and fully quantified.

The landlord should also explain the legal basis for any such claim, i.e. whether it is made as part of the damages claim or under some express or implied provision of the lease.

4.7 The claim should generally contain the following information:

- the landlord's full name and address;
- the tenant's full name and address;
- a clear summary of the facts on which the claim is based;
- the schedule referred to above;
- a clear summary of the monetary sums the landlord is claiming as damages in respect of the breaches. This may include the cost of the works, the consequential costs and fees, VAT, loss of rent and other losses (including any sums paid to a superior landlord);
- any documents relied upon or required by this protocol, including copies of any receipted invoices or other evidence of such costs and losses;
- confirmation that the landlord and/or its professional advisers will attend a meeting or meetings as proposed under section 7 below;
- a date (being a reasonable time) by which the tenant should respond. In the usual case 56 days should be adopted as a reasonable time.

4.8 *Landlord's Loss*

4.8.1 The landlord's claim should be restricted to its loss. This is not necessarily the same as the cost of works to remedy the breaches.

4.8.2 The claim should not include items of work that are not required because they are likely to be superseded by works to be carried out by the landlord at or shortly after the termination of the tenancy or items likely to be superseded by the landlord's intentions for the property at or shortly after the termination of the tenancy (sometimes called "supercession").

4.8.3 In preparing the claim the person preparing it should have regard to the principles laid down in the Royal Institution of Chartered Surveyors' Guidance Note on Dilapidations (if a surveyor) and in any case to the matters set out in paragraph 1.7 above.

4.8.5 A formal quantification of the landlord's loss based on either a formal diminution valuation or an account of the actual expenditure or a combination of both must be provided by the landlord to the tenant prior to issuing proceedings. (See section 10 below.)

5 The Response

5.1 The tenant must respond to the claim within a reasonable time. In the usual case 56 days should be adopted as a reasonable time.

5.2 The tenant should respond using the schedule provided by the landlord, where appropriate, in sufficient detail to enable the landlord to understand clearly the tenant's views on each item of claim.

5.3 The response should take account of what works, in the opinion of the tenant's surveyor, are reasonably required for the tenant to comply with its covenants or obligations, what amount is reasonably payable for such works and what payment is reasonable for the other amounts claimed. It should also take account of what the tenant's surveyor believes to be the landlord's intentions for the property at or shortly after the termination of the tenancy.

5.4 If the tenant's surveyor considers that any items in the claim are likely to be superseded by works to be carried out by the landlord or are likely to be superseded by the landlord's intentions for the property, the surveyor should state this in the response and should give particulars of that on which the surveyor relies, e.g. correspondence or minutes of the landlord company (see 6 below), and the surveyor should also state the items in the landlord's claim to which this view is relevant.

6 Disclosure of Documents

Disclosure will generally be limited to the documents required to be enclosed with the claim letter and the tenant's response. The parties can agree that further disclosure may be given. If either or both of the parties consider that further disclosure should be given but there is disagreement about some aspect of that process, they may be able to make an application for pre-action disclosure under CPR Part 31.

7 Negotiations

7.1 The landlord and tenant and/or their respective professional advisers are encouraged to meet before the tenant is required to respond to the claim and must generally meet within 28 days of service of the tenant's response. The meetings will be without prejudice and preferably on site, to review the schedule to ensure that the tenant understands fully all aspects of the landlord's claim and the parties should seek to agree as many of the items in dispute as possible.

7.2 In a complex matter it may be necessary for more than one site visit or without prejudice meeting between the parties to take place. These ought to be conducted without unnecessary delay.

8 Alternative Dispute Resolution

8.1 The parties should consider whether some form of alternative dispute resolution procedure would be more suitable than litigation, and if so, endeavour to agree which form to adopt. Both the landlord and tenant may be required by the Court to provide evidence that alternative means of resolving their dispute were considered. The Courts take the view that litigation should be a last resort, and that claims should not be issued prematurely when a settlement is still actively being explored. Parties are warned that if the protocol is not followed (including this paragraph) then the Court must have regard to such conduct when determining costs.

8.2 It is not practicable in this protocol to address in detail how the parties might decide which method to adopt to resolve their particular dispute. However, summarised below are some of the options for resolving disputes without litigation:

- Discussion and negotiation.
- Early neutral evaluation by an independent third party (for example, a lawyer experienced in that field or an individual experienced in the subject matter of the claim).
- Mediation – a form of facilitated negotiation assisted by an independent neutral party.

The Legal Services Commission has published a booklet on "Alternatives to Court", CLS Direct Information Leaflet 23 (www.clsdirect.org.uk/legalhelp/leaflet23.jsp), which lists a number of organisations that provide alternative dispute resolution services. The RICS and PLA websites also list a number of experienced mediators.

It is expressly recognised that no party can or should be forced to mediate or enter into any form of ADR.

9 Stocktake

Where a claim is not resolved when the protocol has been followed, the parties might wish to carry out a "stocktake" of the issues in dispute, and the evidence (including technical evidence) that the court is likely to need to decide those issues, before proceedings are started.

10 Formal Diminution Valuation and Quantification of the Claim prior to Issue of Proceedings (NB See flowchart at Annex [B])

10.1.1 Any technical evidence which might be presented to the Court should be prepared in an appropriate manner by an appropriately qualified Expert. Attention is drawn to *Civil Procedure Rules* rule 35.4(1) 'No party may call an expert or put in evidence an expert's report without the Court's permission.' There is a Protocol for the Instruction of Experts to give Evidence in Civil Claims which can be found at: www.dca.gov.uk/civil/procrules_fin/contents/form_section_images/practice_directions/pd35_pdf_eps/pd35_prot.pdf

10.1.2 The landlord must quantify its loss by providing to the tenant a detailed breakdown of the issues and consequential losses based on either a formal diminution valuation or an account of the actual expenditure or a combination of both. For these purposes a formal diminution valuation is a valuation showing the diminution in value to the landlord's reversionary interest in the property due to the fact that the tenant has not complied with its covenants or obligations relating to the physical state of the property.

10.1.3 If a formal diminution valuation is produced it should be prepared by a valuer. Only one valuation is required which takes account of both s. 18(1) in relation to breaches of covenants or obligations to repair, and common law principles of loss for other covenants or obligations.

10.2.1 If the landlord has carried out the work it considers should have been done to remedy the breaches of covenant or obligations, it is not usually required to provide a formal diminution valuation but may base the claim on an account of the actual expenditure. However, the landlord should provide a formal diminution valuation if in all the circumstances it would be reasonable to do so.

10.2.2 If the landlord has carried out some of the work but not all of it, it is not usually required to provide a formal diminution valuation in relation to the work which has been done but may base the claim for those works on an account of the actual expenditure. However, the landlord should provide a formal diminution valuation if in all the circumstances it would be reasonable to do so. With regard to the remaining works it should comply as in 10.2.3 or 10.2.4 below depending on whether or not it intends to carry out those remaining works.

10.2.3 If the landlord has not carried out the work but intends to, it must state when it intends to do the work, and what steps it has taken towards getting the work done, e.g. preparing a specification or bills of quantities or inviting tenders. The scope of the landlord's proposed works should be clearly shown to enable any effect on the dilapidations claim to be identified. The landlord should provide a formal diminution valuation unless, in all the circumstances, it would be reasonable not to.

10.2.4 If the landlord does not intend to carry out the work, then it should provide a formal diminution valuation for comparison with the schedule based claim in order to establish whether the claim is capped by the valuation unless, in all the circumstances, it would be reasonable not to.

10.3 If the tenant relies on a defence on the basis of diminution, it must state its case for so doing and provide a diminution valuation to the landlord. If a formal diminution valuation is produced only one valuation is required which takes account of both s. 18(1) in relation to breaches of covenants or obligations to repair, and common law principles of loss for other covenants or obligations.

10.4 The tenant's diminution valuation shall be served within a reasonable time. A "reasonable time" will vary from case to case but generally will not be more than 56 days after the landlord has served his quantified claim under 10.1.2.

11 Court Proceedings

If the parties cannot reach a settlement after complying with the protocol then the final step will be for the dispute to be referred to the Court.

Annex A: Section 18(1) of the Landlord and Tenant Act 1927

Provisions as to covenants to repair

Damages for a breach of a covenant or agreement to keep or put premises in repair during the currency of a lease, or to leave or put premises in repair at the termination of a lease, whether such covenant or agreement is expressed or implied, and whether general or specific, shall in no case exceed the amount (if any) by which the value of the reversion (whether immediate or not) in the premises is diminished owing to the breach of such covenant or agreement as aforesaid; and in particular no damage shall be recovered for a breach of any such covenant or agreement to leave or put premises in repair at the termination of a lease, if it is shown that the premises, in whatever state of repair they might be, would at or shortly after the termination of the tenancy have been or be pulled down, or such structural alterations made therein as would render valueless the repairs covered by the covenant or agreement.

Annex B

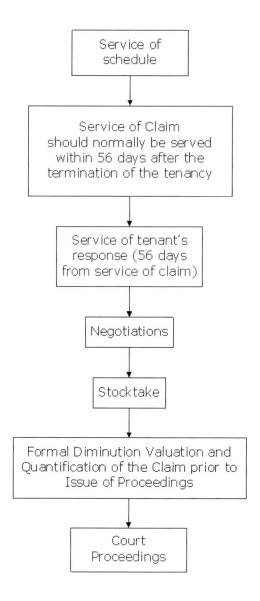

NB:
1. The provisions of this Protocol should be adopted in respect of each of the stages detailed in this flowchart.
2. The parties should consider throughout this process whether ADR would assist in settling the dispute.
3. Service in this context means the issuing of the relevant document to the tenant or landlord by the other party, its surveyor or solicitor as appropriate, and should be in accordance with any provisions laid down in the lease as to service.

Annex C: Schedule of Dilapidations

This schedule has been prepared by [name, individual and firm], upon the instructions of [name the landlord]. It was prepared following [name, i.e. same name as above]'s inspection of the property known as [property] on [date].

It records the works required to be done to the property in order that they are put into the physical state the property should have been put if the tenant [name] had complied with its covenants or obligations contained within its lease of the property dated [   ].

The covenants or obligations of the said lease with which the tenant should have complied are as follows:

>   [Set out clause number of the lease and quote the clause verbatim].

The following schedule contains:

- reference to the specific clause (quoted above) under which the obligation arises,
- the breach complained of,
- the remedial works suggested by the landlord's surveyor [name, i.e. same name as above] as suitable for remedying the breach complained of,
- the landlord's view on the cost of the works.

The schedule contains the true views of [name, i.e. the same name as above] being the surveyor appointed/employed by the landlord to prepare the schedule.

Upon receipt of this schedule the tenant should respond using this schedule in the relevant column below to enable the landlord to understand clearly the tenant's views on each item of claim.

1 Item No.	2 Clause No.	3 Breach complained of	4 Remedial works required	5 Landlord's costings

DATED [..........................]

SIGNED [..........................]

[Name and address of surveyor appointed by landlord]

Appendix B: Example of a schedule of dilapidations

1 Item no.	2 Clause no.	3 Breach complained of	4 Remedial works required	5 Cost
		Car parking area		
1	4(6)(a)	Floodlighting is provided within the planting area to light the front elevation of the building. Floodlight fittings are corroded and broken. None of the 4 No. fittings are in working order.	Renew 4 No. floodlight fittings and check switchgear and wiring.	2,000
2	4(6)(a)	Car parking and hardstanding to east of the north wing. Precast concrete paving slabs to paths adjacent to building. 30 No. slabs are cracked and broken. 50 No. slabs are displaced and uneven.	Take up and dispose of damaged slabs. Lay new slabs to match existing. Take up and re-lay uneven and displaced slabs.	1,600
3	4(6)(a)	Grass covered banks between perimeter paving and footpath to roadway. Grass has died to 25m².	Prepare topsoil base and lay 25m² of new turf.	450
4	4(6)(a)	Gas access chamber adjacent to directors' parking bays. Chamber is damaged.	Repair damaged chamber.	600
5	4(6)(a)	Tarmacadam surfacing to car park areas with thermoplastic markings to car park bays. There is localised damage to tarmac surface including pot holes approx 300mm dia. particularly adjacent to gullies.	Patch repair tarmac to damaged areas (allow 15m²).	875
6	4(6)(a)	The markings to car parking bays are worn and missing in places.	Burn off all residual markings and apply new thermoplastic markings to all parking bays; redesign and set out to standard size parking bays.	3,500
		Internal: ground floor – west wing		
7	4(6)(a)	4 No. new infill bays following removal of tenant blockwork. Glazing not tinted to match existing.	Replace glass with tinted glass – 16 No. windows in total.	3,200
8	4(7)	Versatemp units installed by tenant.	Refix units that have not been securely mounted on external walls.	1,500
9	4(7)	Computer trunking skirting to perimeter. Not laid against the floor leaving uneven gap.	Take up. Refit at lower level to close up the gap; make good finishes; redecorate.	2,750
10	4(7)	Ceiling tiles: damp staining already showing from roof leaks above. 2 No. tiles missing.	Replace missing and damaged tiles.	100
11	4(7)	Smokers' room window frames heavily stained from nicotine, etc.	Replace cover frames left by tenant when this area was formerly a smoking room.	950
12	4(7)	Plasterwork is damp damaged particularly at high level in lobbies adjacent to curtain wall enclosure.	Hack off damp damaged plasterwork and make good. Repair wall surfaces and prepare for redecoration.	3,685
13	4(7)	Decorative finishes to wall surfaces have been damaged and are soiled.	Apply mist coat and two full coats emulsion paint finish to all previously decorated surfaces.	2,025
		Escape stairs to west wing		
14	4(6)(b)	Plasterwork is damp damaged particularly at high level in lobbies adjacent to curtain wall enclosure.	Hack off damp damaged and cracked plasterwork and make good.	3,685
15	4(6)(b)	There is extensive cracking to plastered surfaces.	Hack off damp damaged and cracked plasterwork and make good.	Inc above
16	4(6)(b)	Decorative finishes to wall surfaces have been damaged and are soiled.	Repair wall surfaces and prepare for redecoration. Apply mist coat and two full coats emulsion paint finish to all previously decorated surfaces.	2,025
17	4(6)(b)	Ceiling tiles are generally discoloured. Many tiles are damaged, chipped or stained.	Renew all suspended ceiling tiles (replacement of damaged tiles only will result in a patchy and inconsistent appearance).	3,785
18	4(6)(b)	Carpets have widespread staining as a result of spillages and poor maintenance.	Take up and dispose of all carpet tiles. Supply and lay new carpet tiles of a grade and quality to match existing tiles.	5,600
				38,330

Appendix C: Recommended form of Scott Schedule

SCOTT SCHEDULE – CASE: PROPERTY ADDRESS – CATEGORY OF WORK

1 Item no.	2 Clause no.	3 Breach complained of	4 Remedial works required	5 Tenant's comments	6 Landlord's comments	7 Landlord	8 Tenant
			Subcategory of work described in this section of the sheet				
1						0	0
2						0	0
3						0	0
4						0	0
5						0	0
6						0	0
			Subcategory of work described in this section of the sheet				
7						0	0
8						0	0
9						0	0
10						0	0
11						0	0
12						0	0
13						0	0
			Subcategory of work described in this section of the sheet				
14						0	0
15						0	0
16						0	0
17						0	0
18						0	0
19						0	0
			TOTALS – CATEGORY			0	0

Appendix D: Example of a Scott Schedule

SCOTT SCHEDULE – CASE: STREAMSIDE, ROBIN HOOD WAY, NOTTINGHAM – REPAIR AND DECORATION

1 Item no.	2 Clause no.	3 Breach complained of	4 Remedial works required	5 Tenant's comments	6 Landlord's comments	7 Landlord	8 Tenant
				Car parking area			
1	4(6)(a)	Floodlighting is provided within the planting area to light the front elevation of the building. Floodlight fittings are corroded and broken. None of the 4 No. fittings are in working order.	Renew 4 No. floodlight fittings and check switchgear and wiring.	Item agreed – allow for retubing 4 No. floor light fittings and check electrical wiring to ensure safe operation. Landlord's claim is excessive.	Renewal is closer to the standard contemplated by the covenant.	2,000	1,600
2	4(6)(a)	Car parking and hardstanding to east of the north wing. Precast concrete paving slabs to paths adjacent to building. 30 No. slabs are cracked and broken. 50 No. slabs are displaced and uneven.	Take up and dispose of damaged slabs. Lay new slabs to match existing. Take up and re-lay uneven and displaced slabs.	Item agreed – numerous broken and displaced precast concrete paving flags are noted to the access path to the north wing east elevation. Landlord's claim is excessive.	£1,200 will not meet the requisite standard.	1,600	1,200
3	4(6)(a)	Grass covered banks between perimeter paving and footpath to roadway. Grass has died to 25m².	Prepare topsoil base and lay 25m² of new turf.	At the time of the lease term expiry an area of approximately 25m² of the grassed area was noted to be bare and/or missing. The landlord has failed to maintain the condition of the soft landscaping since lease expiry in January 2002. The soft landscaping is now heavily weed growth affected. Landlord's claim is excessive. The tenants should pay only a contribution towards the reinstatement of the landscaping back to the condition as witnessed at lease term expiry.	The grassed area should have been put into and kept in the condition contemplated by the covenant.	450	450
4	4(6)(a)	Gas access chamber adjacent to directors' parking bays. Chamber is damaged.	Repair damaged chamber.	A small gas chamber is located within the paving flag access path adjacent to the directors' car park. Extremely minor impact damage is noted to the concrete haunching/bedding to the gas chamber housing. Landlord's claim is excessive.	The minor damage nonetheless requires a major repair.	600	100
5	4(6)(a)	Tarmacadam surfacing to car park areas with thermoplastic markings to car park bays. There is localised damage to tarmac surface including pot holes approx 300mm dia. particularly adjacent to gullies.	Patch repair tarmac to damaged areas (allow 15m²).	Item disagreed – generally the tarmacadam hardstanding is in reasonable order with the exception of small number of pot holes. The areas identified on the landlord's schedule (15m²) are excessive. Approximately 10 No. pot holes to all car parks require attention in order to return them into a good condition. Landlord's claim is excessive. Allow for making good 10 No. pot holes size approx 500m² by 150mm deep.	Agreed, and cost reduction agreed.	875	875

1 Item no.	2 Clause no.	3 Breach complained of	4 Remedial works required	5 Tenant's comments	6 Landlord's comments	7 Landlord	8 Tenant
6	4(6)(a)	The markings to car parking bays are worn and missing in places.	Burn off all residual markings and apply new thermoplastic markings to all parking bays; redesign and set out to standard size parking bays	Item agreed – the road markings to the rear car park area are aged, weathered and require to be renewed. The landlord's claim is excessive.	£2,500 will not meet the requisite standard.	3,500	2,500
		Internal: ground floor – west wing					
7	4(6)(a)	4 No. new infill bays following removal of tenant blockwork. Glazing not tinted to match existing.	Replace glass with tinted glass – 16 No. windows in total.	Item agreed – the glazing panes to the new replacement curtain walling to the ground floor west wing does not match the tint and colour of the original curtain walling sections.	Agreed.	3,200	3,200
8	4(7)	Versatemp units installed by tenant.	Refix units that have not been securely mounted on external walls	Item agreed.	Agreed.	1,500	1,500
9	4(7)	Computer trunking skirting to perimeter – not laid against the floor leaving uneven gap.	Take up. Refit at lower level to close up the gap; make good finishes; redecorate.	A nominal gap between the floor slab and underside of the new electrical skirting trunking is noted. The new skirting trunking installed at the time of the reinstatement works has been lined through with the head of the original skirting trunking in situ to provide an even finish to the floor plate. Electrical skirting trunking is operable and has been provided with test certification. Therefore no breach of covenant or disrepair has been identified by the landlord. Allow for providing cloaking piece to base of new infill sections of skirting trunking.	Agreed, but cost would be £750.	2,750	2,000
10	4(7)	Ceiling tiles: damp staining already showing from roof leaks above. 2 No. tiles missing.	Replace missing and damaged tiles.	Item agreed. Cost excessive.	£100 reasonable.	100	20
11	4(7)	Smokers' room window frames heavily stained from nicotine, etc.	Replace cover frames left by tenant when this area was formerly a smoking room.	Location not identified – landlord to provide further evidence as to location and breach of covenant or disrepair identified.	To follow.	950	n/a

1 Item no.	2 Clause no.	3 Breach complained of	4 Remedial works required	5 Tenant's comments	6 Landlord's comments	7 Landlord	8 Tenant
12	4(7)	Plasterwork is damp damaged particularly at high level in lobbies adjacent to curtain wall enclosure.	Hack off damp damaged plasterwork and make good. Repair wall surfaces and prepare for redecoration.	Areas of damp and rainwater penetration have been recorded within the main stairwell at high level around the junction of curtain walling and flat roof soffit. We anticipate that there is an approximate 5m² in total patch repairs to be undertaken to the plaster finishes throughout this area. The landlord's claim and costs are excessive.	The area in question is more like 12m².	3,685	2,950
13	4(7)	Decorative finishes to wall surfaces have been damaged and are soiled.	Apply mist coat and two full coats emulsion paint finish to all previously decorated surfaces.	Tenant is under an obligation in the last year of the term to redecorate.	Agreed.	2,025	2,025
Escape stairs to west wing							
14	4(6)(b)	Plasterwork is damp damaged particularly at high level in lobbies adjacent to curtain wall enclosure.	Hack off damp damaged and cracked plasterwork and make good.	Approximately 20m² in total patch repairs of rainwater affected loose and off key plaster finishes are recorded. Landlord's claim excessive.	Area is about 60m².	3,685	800
15	4(6)(b)	There is extensive cracking to plastered surfaces.	Hack off damp damaged and cracked plasterwork and make good.	Landlord's claim and costs are excessive. Refer to item 14 above. Cost included in item 14.	See above	Inc above	Inc above
16	4(6)(b)	Decorative finishes to wall surfaces have been damaged and are soiled.	Repair wall surfaces and prepare for redecoration. Apply mist coat and two full coats emulsion paint finish to all previously decorated surfaces.	Item agreed – tenant is under an obligation to redecorate within the last year of the term.	Agreed.	2,025	2,025
17	4(6)(b)	Ceiling tiles are generally discoloured. Many tiles are damaged, chipped or stained.	Renew all suspended ceiling tiles (replacement of damaged tiles only will result in a patchy and inconsistent appearance).	Refer to item 6.2.1. No disrepair accepted.	Disrepair is significant.	3,785	0
18	4(6)(b)	Carpets have widespread staining as a result of spillages and poor maintenance.	Take up and dispose of all carpet tiles. Supply and lay new carpet tiles of a grade and quality to match existing tiles.	Item agreed – carpet tile finish within west wing stairwell is aged and worn. Landlord's claim is excessive.	Agreed and reduced cost agreed.	5,600	4,200
						38,330	25,445

Appendix E: Value Added Tax

1   The question of whether a landlord can properly claim VAT as part of its damages claim often arises.

2   A sum equivalent to the VAT paid (or likely to be paid) is recoverable as damages where the landlord does, or intends to do, work the tenant failed to do and pays, or will pay, VAT on those works but is unable to offset that VAT as input tax.

3   Generally, the services required by a landlord from contractors and professional advisers to deal with dilapidations will be standard rated 'supplies'. So those contractors and advisers will (unless they are very small businesses) add VAT to the charge for their services; a VAT charge will, therefore, be incurred by the landlord.

4   Whether that VAT charge can be offset by the landlord as an input depends on its own tax position and the nature of the property. The precise details of the circumstances in which a landlord will be able to offset its VAT charge is beyond the scope of this note. However, what can be said is that, if the landlord is unable to offset (in part or whole) the VAT charge, then an amount equivalent to the VAT paid that cannot be offset can properly be added to the damages claim. Conversely, if a landlord can fully offset the VAT charge as input tax against any output tax it charges (or can otherwise recover the input tax from HM Revenue & Customs (HMRC)), then it will not have suffered a loss as a consequence of the VAT input charge. In this latter situation, the landlord cannot properly reclaim an equivalent amount as damages from the tenant.

5   It is for the landlord to demonstrate that it cannot offset the VAT charge for whatever reason.

6   A further question that often arises is whether a tenant can require the landlord to provide a VAT invoice in respect of the dilapidations payment it makes to the landlord.

7   HMRC has given clear guidance (see Notice 742 *Land and Property*, paragraph 10.10) that a dilapidations claim represents a claim for damages by the landlord against the tenant and that the payment involved is not the consideration for a 'supply' for VAT purposes and so is outside the scope of VAT. Thus, no VAT invoice can properly be raised. As a consequence, the tenant, even if VAT registered, cannot offset or reclaim from HMRC the VAT element of the damages payment to the landlord.

8   In view of this, if the landlord cannot offset or reclaim its VAT, there could be a financial advantage to a VAT registered tenant in undertaking dilapidations works before the end of the term. The tenant might then be able to offset the input tax that its contractors and professional advisers charge against its output tax. By doing the works, the tenant would avoid liability for damages equivalent to the landlord's VAT charge that it could not treat as input tax.

Appendix F: Extracts from legislation

The following extracts from legislation are reproduced in this appendix:

- *Law of Property Act* 1925 – section 146;

- *Landlord and Tenant Act* 1927 – section 18;

- *Leasehold Property (Repairs) Act* 1938 – sections 1–8;

- *Landlord and Tenant Act* 1954 – section 51.

The extracts are as amended by subsequent legislation as noted on the UK Statute Law database. Amendments are in square brackets.

Crown copyright material is reproduced with the permission of the Controller of HMSO and the Queen's Printer for Scotland.

An online database of revised UK primary legislation can be found at www.statutelaw.gov.uk, the UK Statute Law Database (SLD). The database is the official revised edition of UK primary legislation online. It contains primary legislation that was in force at 1 February 1991 and primary and secondary legislation that has been produced since that date. Note that there may be amendments which have not yet been applied. See the status statement at the top of each piece of legislation.

UK legislation passed after 1988 is published in its original form by the Office of Public Sector Information at www.opsi.gov.uk and UK legislation prior to 1988 may be purchased through the Stationery Office Limited on www.tso.co.uk

Law of Property Act 1925

Part V: Leases and tenancies

146 Restrictions on and relief against forfeiture of leases and underleases

(1) A right of re-entry or forfeiture under any provisio or stipulation in a lease for a breach of any covenant or condition in the lease shall not be enforceable, by action or otherwise, unless and until the lessor serves on the lessee a notice:

(a) specifying the particular breach complained of; and

(b) if the breach is capable of remedy, requiring the lessee to remedy the breach; and

(c) in any case, requiring the lessee to make compensation in money for the breach;

and the lessee fails, within a reasonable time thereafter, to remedy the breach, if it is capable of remedy, and to make reasonable compensation in money, to the satisfaction of the lessor, for the breach.

(2) Where a lessor is proceeding, by action or otherwise, to enforce such a right of re-entry or forfeiture, the lessee may, in the lessor's action, if any, or in any action brought by himself, apply to the court for relief; and the court may grant or refuse relief, as the court, having regard to the proceedings and conduct of the parties under the foregoing provisions of

this section, and to all the other circumstances, thinks fit; and in case of relief may grant it on such terms, if any, as to costs, expenses, damages, compensation, penalty, or otherwise, including the granting of an injunction to restrain any like breach in the future, as the court, in the circumstances of each case, thinks fit.

(3) A lessor shall be entitled to recover as a debt due to him from a lessee, and in addition to damages (if any), all reasonable costs and expenses properly incurred by the lessor in the employment of a solicitor and surveyor or valuer, or otherwise, in reference to any breach giving rise to a right of re-entry or forfeiture which, at the request of the lessee, is waived by the lessor, or from which the lessee is relieved, under the provisions of this Act.

(4) Where a lessor is proceeding by action or otherwise to enforce a right of re-entry or forfeiture under any covenant, proviso, or stipulation in a lease, or for non-payment of rent, the court may, on application by any person claiming as under-lessee any estate or interest in the property comprised in the lease or any part thereof, either in the lessor's action (if any) or in any action brought by such person for that purpose, make an order vesting, for the whole term of the lease or any less term, the property comprised in the lease or any part thereof in any person entitled as under-lessee to any estate or interest in such property upon such conditions as to execution of any deed or other document, payment of rent, costs, expenses, damages, compensation, giving security, or otherwise, as the court in the circumstances of each case may think fit, but in no case shall any such under-lessee be entitled to require a lease to be granted to him for any longer term than he had under his original sub-lease.

(5) For the purposes of this section:

(a) "Lease" includes an original or derivative under-lease; also an agreement for a lease where the lessee has become entitled to have his lease granted; also a grant at a fee farm rent, or securing a rent by condition;

(b) "Lessee" includes an original or derivative under-lessee, and the persons deriving title under a lessee; also a grantee under any such grant as aforesaid and the persons deriving title under him;

(c) "Lessor" includes an original or derivative under-lessor, and the persons deriving title under a lessor; also a person making such grant as aforesaid and the persons deriving title under him;

(d) "Under-lease" includes an agreement for an under-lease where the under-lessee has become entitled to have his under-lease granted;

(e) "Under-lessee" includes any person deriving title under an under-lessee.

(6) This section applies although the proviso or stipulation under which the right of re-entry or forfeiture accrues is inserted in the lease in pursuance of the directions of any Act of Parliament.

(7) For the purposes of this section a lease limited to continue as long only as the lessee abstains from committing a breach of covenant shall be and take effect as a lease to continue for any longer term for which it could subsist, but determinable by a proviso for re-entry on such a breach.

(8) This section does not extend:

(i) To a covenant or condition against assigning, underletting, parting with the possession, or disposing of the land leased where the breach occurred before the commencement of this Act; or

(ii) In the case of a mining lease, to a covenant or condition for allowing the lessor to have access to or inspect books, accounts, records, weighing machines or other things, or to enter or inspect the mine or the workings thereof.

(9) This section does not apply to a condition for forfeiture on the bankruptcy of the lessee or on taking in execution of the lessee's interest if contained in a lease of:

(a) Agricultural or pastoral land;

(b) Mines or minerals;

(c) A house used or intended to be used as a public-house or beershop;

(d) A house let as a dwelling-house, with the use of any furniture, books, works of art, or other chattels not being in the nature of fixtures;

(e) Any property with respect to which the personal qualifications of the tenant are of importance for the preservation of the value or character of the property, or on the ground of neighbourhood to the lessor, or to any person holding under him.

(10) Where a condition of forfeiture on the bankruptcy of the lessee or on taking in execution of the lessee's interest is contained in any lease, other than a lease of any of the classes mentioned in the last sub-section, then:

(a) if the lessee's interest is sold within one year from the bankruptcy or taking in execution, this section applies to the forfeiture condition aforesaid;

(b) if the lessee's interest is not sold before the expiration of that year, this section only applies to the forfeiture condition aforesaid during the first year from the date of the bankruptcy or taking in execution.

(11) This section does not, save as otherwise mentioned, affect the law relating to re-entry or forfeiture or relief in case of non-payment of rent.

(12) This section has effect notwithstanding any stipulation to the contrary.

(13) [The county court has jurisdiction under this section.]

Landlord and Tenant Act 1927

Part II: General amendments of the law of landlord and tenant

18 Provisions as to covenants to repair

(1) Damages for a breach of a covenant or agreement to keep or put premises in repair during the currency of a lease, or to leave or put premises in repair at the termination of a lease, whether such covenant or agreement is expressed or implied, and whether general or specific, shall in no case exceed the amount (if any) by which the value of the reversion (whether immediate or not) in the premises is diminished owing to the breach of such covenant or agreement as aforesaid; and in particular no damage shall be recovered for a breach of any such covenant or agreement to leave or put premises in repair at the termination of a lease, if it is shown that the premises, in whatever state of repair they might be, would at or shortly

after the termination of the tenancy have been or be pulled down, or such structural alterations made therein as would render valueless the repairs covered by the covenant or agreement.

(2) A right of re-entry or forfeiture for a breach of any such covenant or agreement as aforesaid shall not be enforceable, by action or otherwise, unless the lessor proves that the fact that such a notice as is required by section one hundred and forty-six of the Law of Property Act, 1925, had been served on the lessee was known either:

(a) to the lessee; or

(b) to an under-lessee holding under an under-lease which reserved a nominal reversion only to the lessee; or

(c) to the person who last paid the rent due under the lease either on his own behalf or as agent for the lessee or under-lessee;

and that a time reasonably sufficient to enable the repairs to be executed had elapsed since the time when the fact of the service of the notice came to the knowledge of any such person.

Where a notice has been sent by registered post addressed to a person at his last known place of abode in the United Kingdom, then, for the purposes of this subsection, that person shall be deemed, unless the contrary is proved, to have had knowledge of the fact that the notice had been served as from the time at which the letter would have been delivered in the ordinary course of post.

This subsection shall be construed as one with section one hundred and forty-six of the Law of Property Act, 1925.

(3) This section applies whether the lease was created before or after the commencement of this Act.

Leasehold Property (Repairs) Act 1938

1 Restriction on enforcement of repairing covenants in long leases of small houses

(1) Where a lessor serves on a lessee under subsection (1) of section one hundred and forty-six of the Law of Property Act, 1925, a notice that relates to a breach of a covenant or agreement to keep or put in repair during the currency of the lease [all or any of the property comprised in the lease], and at the date of the service of the notice [three] years or more of the term of the lease remain unexpired, the lessee may within twenty-eight days from that date serve on the lessor a counter-notice to the effect that he claims the benefit of this Act.

(2) A right to damages for a breach of such a covenant as aforesaid shall not be enforceable by action commenced at any time at which [three] years or more of the term of the lease remain unexpired unless the lessor has served on the lessee not less than one month before the commencement of the action such a notice as is specified in subsection (1) of section one hundred and forty-six of the Law of Property Act, 1925, and where a notice is served under this subsection, the lessee may, within twenty-eight days from the date of the service thereof, serve on the lessor a counter-notice to the effect that he claims the benefit of this Act.

(3) Where a counter-notice is served by a lessee under this section, then, notwithstanding anything in any enactment or rule of law, no

proceedings, by action or otherwise, shall be taken by the lessor for the enforcement of any right of re-entry or forfeiture under any proviso or stipulation in the lease for breach of the covenant or agreement in question, or for damages for breach thereof, otherwise than with the leave of the court.

(4) A notice served under subsection (1) of section one hundred and forty-six of the Law of Property Act, 1925, in the circumstances specified in subsection (1) of this section, and a notice served under subsection (2) of this section shall not be valid unless it contains a statement, in characters not less conspicuous than those used in any other part of the notice, to the effect that the lessee is entitled under this Act to serve on the lessor a counter-notice claiming the benefit of this Act, and a statement in the like characters specifying the time within which, and the manner in which, under this Act a counter-notice may be served and specifying the name and address for service of the lessor.

(5) Leave for the purposes of this section shall not be given unless the lessor proves:

(a) that the immediate remedying of the breach in question is requisite for preventing substantial diminution in the value of his reversion, or that the value thereof has been substantially diminished by the breach;

(b) that the immediate remedying of the breach is required for giving effect in relation to the [premises] to the purposes of any enactment, or of any byelaw or other provision having effect under an enactment, [or for giving effect to any order of a court or requirement of any authority under any enactment or any such byelaw or other provision as aforesaid];

(c) in a case in which the lessee is not in occupation of the whole of the [premises as respects which the covenant or agreement is proposed to be enforced], that the immediate remedying of the breach is required in the interests of the occupier of [those premises] or of part thereof;

(d) that the breach can be immediately remedied at an expense that is relatively small in comparison with the much greater expense that would probably be occasioned by postponement of the necessary work; or

(e) special circumstances which in the opinion of the court, render it just and equitable that leave should be given.

(6) The court may, in granting or in refusing leave for the purposes of this section, impose such terms and conditions on the lessor or on the lessee as it may think fit.

2 Restriction on right to recover expenses of survey, etc.

A lessor on whom a counter-notice is served under the preceding section shall not be entitled to the benefit of subsection (3) of section one hundred and forty-six of the Law of Property Act, 1925, (which relates to costs and expenses incurred by a lessor in reference to breaches of covenant), so far as regards any costs or expenses incurred in reference to the breach in question, unless he makes an application for leave for the purposes of the preceding section, and on such an application the court shall have power to direct whether and to what extent the lessor is to be entitled to the benefit thereof.

3 Saving for obligation to repair on taking possession

This Act shall not apply to a breach of a covenant or agreement in so far as it imposes on the lessee an obligation to put [premises] in repair that is to be performed upon the lessee taking possession of the premises or within a reasonable time thereafter.

4 [Repealed]

5 Application to past breaches

This Act applies to leases created, and to breaches occurring, before or after the commencement of this Act.

6 Court having jurisdiction under this Act

(1) In this Act the expression "the court" means the county court, except in a case in which any proceedings by action for which leave may be given would have to be taken in a court other than the county court, and means in the said excepted case that other court.

(2) [Repealed]

7 Application of certain provisions of 15 and 16 Geo. 5 c. 20

(1) In this Act the expressions "lessor", "lessee" and "lease" have the meanings assigned to them respectively by sections one hundred and forty-six and one hundred and fifty-four of the Law of Property Act, 1925, except that they do not include any reference to such a grant as is mentioned in the said section one hundred and forty-six, or to the person making, or to the grantee under such a grant, or to persons deriving title under such a person; and "lease" means a lease for a term of [seven years or more, not being a lease of an agricultural holding within the meaning of the [Agricultural Holdings Act 1986]] [which is a lease in relation to which that Act applies and not being a farm business tenancy within the meaning of the Agricultural Tenancies Act 1995].

(2) The provisions of section one hundred and ninety-six of the said Act (which relate to the service of notices) shall extend to notices and counter-notices required or authorised by this Act.

8 Short title and extent

(1) This Act may be cited as the Leasehold Property (Repairs) Act, 1938.

(2) This Act shall not extend to Scotland or to Northern Ireland.

Landlord and Tenant Act 1954

Part IV: Miscellaneous and supplementary

51 Extension of Leasehold Property (Repairs) Act 1938

(1) The Leasehold Property (Repairs) Act 1938 (which restricts the enforcement of repairing covenants in long leases of small houses) shall extend to every tenancy (whether of a house or of other property, and without regard to rateable value) where the following conditions are fulfilled, that is to say:

(a) that the tenancy was granted for a term of years certain of not less than seven years;

(b) that three years or more of the term remain unexpired at the date of the service of the notice of dilapidations or, as the case may be, at the date of commencement of the action for damages; and

(c) [that the tenancy is neither a tenancy of an agricultural holding in relation to which the Agricultural Holdings Act 1986 applies nor a farm business tenancy].

(2) ...

(3) The said Act of 1938 shall apply where there is an interest belonging to Her Majesty in right of the Crown or to a Government department, or held on behalf of Her Majesty for the purposes of a Government department, in like manner as if that interest were an interest not so belonging or held.

(4) Subsection (2) of section twenty-three of the Landlord and Tenant Act 1927 (which authorises a tenant to serve documents on the person to whom he has been paying rent) shall apply in relation to any counter-notice to be served under the said Act of 1938.

(5) This section shall apply to tenancies granted, and to breaches occurring, before or after the commencement of this Act, except that it shall not apply where the notice of dilapidations was served, or the action for damages begun, before the commencement of this Act.

(6) In this section the expression "notice of dilapidations" means a notice under subsection (1) of section one hundred and forty-six of the Law of Property Act 1925.

Appendix G: Paragraph 4 of the CPR Practice Direction on Protocols

The CPR Practice Direction on Protocols can be found at: www.justice.gov.uk/civil/procrules_fin/menus/protocol.htm

Crown copyright material is reproduced with the permission of the Controller of HMSO and the Queen's Printer for Scotland.

Pre-action behaviour in other cases

4.1 In cases not covered by any approved protocol, the court will expect the parties, in accordance with the overriding objective and the matters referred to in CPR 1.1(2)(a), (b) and (c), to act reasonably in exchanging information and documents relevant to the claim and generally in trying to avoid the necessity for the start of proceedings.

4.2 Parties to a potential dispute should follow a reasonable procedure, suitable to their particular circumstances, which is intended to avoid litigation. The procedure should not be regarded as a prelude to inevitable litigation. It should normally include:

(a) the claimant writing to give details of the claim;

(b) the defendant acknowledging the claim letter promptly;

(c) the defendant giving within a reasonable time a detailed written response; and

(d) the parties conducting genuine and reasonable negotiations with a view to settling the claim economically and without court proceedings.

4.3 The claimant's letter should:

(a) give sufficient concise details to enable the recipient to understand and investigate the claim without extensive further information;

(b) enclose copies of the essential documents which the claimant relies on;

(c) ask for a prompt acknowledgement of the letter, followed by a full written response within a reasonable stated period;

(For many claims, a normal reasonable period for a full response may be one month.)

(d) state whether court proceedings will be issued if the full response is not received within the stated period;

(e) identify and ask for copies of any essential documents, not in his possession, which the claimant wishes to see;

(f) state (if this is so) that the claimant wishes to enter into mediation or another alternative method of dispute resolution; and

(g) draw attention to the court's powers to impose sanctions for failure to comply with this practice direction and, if the recipient is likely to be unrepresented, enclose a copy of this practice direction.

4.4 The defendant should acknowledge the claimant's letter in writing within 21 days of receiving it. The acknowledgement should state when the defendant will give a full written response. If the time for this is longer than the period stated by the claimant, the defendant should give reasons why a longer period is needed.

4.5   The defendant's full written response should as appropriate:

(a)   accept the claim in whole or in part and make proposals for settlement; or

(b)   state that the claim is not accepted.

If the claim is accepted in part only, the response should make clear which part is accepted and which part is not accepted.

4.6   If the defendant does not accept the claim or part of it, the response should:

(a)   give detailed reasons why the claim is not accepted, identifying which of the claimant's contentions are accepted and which are in dispute;

(b)   enclose copies of the essential documents which the defendant relies on;

(c)   enclose copies of documents asked for by the claimant, or explain why they are not enclosed;

(d)   identify and ask for copies of any further essential documents, not in his possession, which the defendant wishes to see; and

   (The claimant should provide these within a reasonably short time or explain in writing why he is not doing so.)

(e)   state whether the defendant is prepared to enter into mediation or another alternative method of dispute resolution.

4.7   The parties should consider whether some form of alternative dispute resolution procedure would be more suitable than litigation, and if so, endeavour to agree which form to adopt. Both the Claimant and Defendant may be required by the Court to provide evidence that alternative means of resolving their dispute were considered. The Courts take the view that litigation should be a last resort, and that claims should not be issued prematurely when a settlement is still actively being explored. Parties are warned that if this paragraph is not followed then the court must have regard to such conduct when determining costs.

It is not practicable in this Practice Direction to address in detail how the parties might decide which method to adopt to resolve their particular dispute. However, summarised below are some of the options for resolving disputes without litigation:

● Discussion and negotiation.

● Early neutral evaluation by an independent third party (for example, a lawyer experienced in that field or an individual experienced in the subject matter of the claim).

● Mediation – a form of facilitated negotiation assisted by an independent neutral party.

The Legal Services Commission has published a booklet on 'Alternatives to Court', CLS Direct Information Leaflet 23 (www.clsdirect.org.uk/legalhelp/leaflet23.jsp), which lists a number of organisations that provide alternative dispute resolution services.

It is expressly recognised that no party can or should be forced to mediate or enter into any form of ADR.

4.8   Documents disclosed by either party in accordance with this practice direction may not be used for any purpose other than resolving the dispute, unless the other party agrees.

4.9   The resolution of some claims, but by no means all, may need help from an expert. If an expert is needed, the parties should wherever possible and to save expense engage an agreed expert.

4.10   Parties should be aware that, if the matter proceeds to litigation, the court may not allow the use of an expert's report, and that the cost of it is not always recoverable.

Acknowledgments

The fifth edition of the RICS *Dilapidations* guidance note was produced by the *Dilapidations Working Group*. RICS wishes to express its sincere thanks to the working group members:

- Alan Beckett, BA (Hons) FRICS DipProjMan

- Peter Beckett, FRICS

- Nicholas Eden, FRICS MCIArb

- Vivien King, HonRICS

- Milton McIntosh, BSc MRICS Solicitor

- Edward Shaw, BSc MSc MRICS

- Stephen Southern, BSc (Hons) DipBdgCons MRICS

- Bartle Woolhouse, BSc (Hons) MRICS

- Kevin Woudman, FRICS FCIArb MAE

Thanks also go to Hugh Love of PWC for his contributions to the VAT appendix.